THE PROVIDENTIAL ROAD TO PURPOSE

MONIKA HARRISON

Cover and interior formatting by KUHN Design Group | kuhndesigngroup.com

Edited by Robin Reed

The Providential Road to Purpose
Seven practical precepts that will transform your life driving you to your kingdom destiny

Copyright © 2025 by Monika Harrison

All rights reserved. This book or any portion thereof may not be reproduced or used in any manner whatsoever without the express written permission of the publisher except for the use of brief quotations in a book review.

ISBN: 979-8-9943508-0-5 (paperback)
ISBN: 979-8-9943508-2-9 (hardcover)
ISBN 979-8-9943508-1-2 (ebook)

Printed in the United States of America

PRAISE FOR PROVIDENTIAL ROAD TO PURPOSE

"*The Providential Road to Purpose* is a book that will encourage and inspire you as it points you to see yourself and the world as God sees you. The writing is rich with biblical truth and scripture and Monika has a unique way of connecting that truth with real human experience through sharing her own heart and vulnerabilities. This book is sure to provide clarity and encouragement as you seek to step into your God given identity and purpose."

— **Julie Wolf, MA**, Licensed Mental Health Counselor
Founder/Owner of Hope Counseling Clinic

"After years of walking closely with Monika, I have witnessed a rich and authentic spiritual life marked by devotion to God, a deep love for people, and a lived commitment to the power of His Word. In seasons of growth, surrender, and faithful obedience, her life has consistently reflected a woman who listens for the voice of the Lord and courageously responds. Her passion for supporting, nurturing, and loving women flows naturally from her own walk with Jesus, creating space for others to encounter healing, freedom, and purpose in His presence. I am confident you will find *The Providential Road to Purpose* both enlightening and empowering—a Spirit-led journey that invites women into a deeper love for our Lord Jesus Christ through her seven A's and three M's, offering wisdom, encouragement, and practical insight for discovering God's providential leading in every season of life."

— **Jacki Farley Founder of Umbwella's Stand**, a nonprofit ministry dedicated to supporting current and future missionaries by empowering followers of Jesus Christ to live in relationship with and operate in the full power of the gospel

"Monika Harrison is a remarkable biblical teacher and a true woman of faith. Her life and ministry radiate a sincere love for God and a deep commitment to seeing believers walk confidently in their Kingdom calling. She has a rare gift for making Scripture come alive in a way that is both spiritually rich and wonderfully practical.

In *The Providential Road to Purpose*, Monika guides readers through seven powerful precepts that gently lead the heart back to God's providential plan. Each page is infused with encouragement, wisdom, and the steady reminder that our lives are not accidental—they are intentionally designed by a faithful God.

This book will strengthen faith, awaken calling, and inspire readers to walk boldly in their Kingdom purpose."

— **Jaylene Rodriguez-Garau**,
Christlit Award–Winning Author, *Creating Our Eden*

"Watching her step into authorship has been such a joy. She is a leader who honors God, loves children fiercely, and leads with compassion and integrity. This book captures her heart and her faith beautifully. I'm confident it will bless and inspire every reader. I am proud to call you my friend Monika, and may God bless you in all the things you will ever do."

— **Chloe Johnson**, Winter Garden City Commissioner, District 3, Director of Community Relations, Eight Waves, Founder & CEO, I AM HER W.E.M. Inc.

"I fondly remember the day Monika Harrison walked into my counseling office and bravely shared the challenges she was facing. As I guided her through The Steps to Freedom, I did not realize she would become an integral part of our lay counseling community, our women's ministry, and my own circle of supporters.

Monika possesses a rare passion for seeing women not only come to know Christ but become rooted in Scripture and walk in the freedom He provides. Her work, "*The Providential Road to Purpose*," is a beautifully written and well-designed discipleship tool. It will enable Christ followers to discover the powerful freedom they have in Him and find their own unique purpose and calling."

—**Deb Moline**, Owner, Extending Hope Central FL, Former Director of Counseling and Recovery at Mosaic Church

"Monika offers a thoughtful and intentional guide that feels like a conversation with a close friend over coffee. If you're seeking a reminder of God's purpose in your life and a moment for meaningful reflection, this book is an invitation to stop, be still, and focus on what really matters."

—**Kerri-Ann Hayes**, Ministry Coach and Consultant, Author of *The Accessible Church*

"Praise be to my Lord and Savior Jesus Christ. God's mercy and grace have carried me through this journey of faith. To Him who is able to do immeasurably more than all we ask or imagine, according to His power that is at work within us (Ephesians 3:20), I give all the glory. This book was born out of a desire to honor God and serve His people. Any wisdom found within these pages belongs to the Holy Spirit; any errors are entirely my own. May this work be an offering—a 'living sacrifice'—unto the Lord, used for His kingdom and His fame."

To my loving and faithful husband—my partner in faith and my best friend, Steve. Thank you for standing by me through every season of life with love, grace, and support. You are a living testimony of God's faithfulness and steadfast love. I love you forever.

To my children, Jasmine and Joshua: Always remember that "The steadfast love of the Lord never ceases; his mercies never come to an end; they are new every morning" (Lamentations 3:22–23). May you wake up every day aware of His love and grace toward you. To my spiritual mentors, Jacki Farley, Deb Moline, and the late Orin Begg: Thank you for your prayers, biblical wisdom, guidance, and encouragement. You taught me how to walk and live out my faith boldly.

CONTENTS

Author's Note 11

How to Pilgrimage Through This Book 13

Introduction 15

WEEK 1: AWARENESS

Day 1: The Goodness of God: Even When Life Is Hard 25

Day 2: The Battle for Your Mind: Finding Freedom in Christ 29

Day 3: From Burden to Blessing: The Path to Spiritual Rest 35

Day 4: Take Up Your Cross: A Call to Faith 39

Day 5: Forgive, Forget, Fix: A Godly Strategy 43

Day 6: Destined for Divine Purpose 47

Day 7: Let Go, Let God: Finding Peace in His Perfect Plan 51

WEEK 2: AGREEMENT

Day 1: The Key to God's Promises: Walking in Obedience 57

Day 2: Reverent Fear: The Foundation of Wisdom and Contentment 61

Day 3: From Bondage to Blessing: Embracing God's Truth 65

Day 4: Living by the Spirit: Obedience, Transformation, and Fruitfulness . . 69

Day 5: From Suffering to Spiritual Growth: Embracing God's Will 73

Day 6: Finding Joy in What You Have: A Lesson in Faith and Provision . . 77

Day 7: Resting in God's Goodness and Grace 81

WEEK 3: ABILITY

Day 1: A Well of Hope, Peace, and Joy 87

Day 2: Facing Your Goliath 91

Day 3: He Is Bigger Than Your Storm 97

Day 4: A Gift of Gratitude 101

Day 5: Living by Faith: A Gift and a Journey 105

Day 6: A Call to Stillness: Resting in the Lord 109

Day 7: Your Daily Weapon: The Armor of God 113

WEEK 4: ABANDONMENT

Day 1: The Blessed Life: Surrendering to God's Will 121

Day 2: Replacing Fear with Faith: A Path to Freedom 125

Day 3: "It Is Finished": The Foundation of Grace 129

Day 4: The Call to Agape: Loving Like Jesus 133

Day 5: Letting Go: Finding Healing Through Forgiveness 139

Day 6: Prayer and Provision: Aligning Your Life with God's Will 145

Day 7: The Power of Mercy: Reflecting God's Love in a Broken World . . 149

WEEK 5: ADORATION

Day 1: Called to Shine: Living As an Ambassador for Christ 155

Day 2: Serving Others: A Path to Peace 161

Day 3: Gratitude: Medicine for the Soul and Fuel for Service 165

Day 4: The Unseen Hand: God's Refining Love 169

Day 5: Never Stop Praying: Your Harvest Awaits 175

Day 6: When God Sings over You: Discovering His Joy and
Unfailing Love 179

Day 7: Praise Anyway: A Song of Peace 183

WEEK 6: ACTION

Day 1: The Power of Your Pain 189

Day 2: The Good Thing: Sustenance for a Serving Heart 193

Day 3: Living for His Kingdom: The Fruit of a Surrendered Life 197

Day 4: Trusting God Through the Whirlwind: Finding Peace in
Uncertainty 203

Day 5: Embrace Your New Beginning: Be Your Light 207

Day 6: God's Masterpiece: Trusting His Pen in the Story of Your Life . . . 211

Day 7: The Unstoppable Flame: The Power of Intimacy 215

WEEK 7: AIM

Day 1: A Spiritual Awakening: Finding Lasting Fire for the Lord 221

Day 2: Breathing Life: Becoming God's Voice of Encouragement 225

Day 3: Hearing His Voice: The Holy Spirit and Your Journey of Faith . . . 229

Day 4: Praise Through the Pain: Finding Purpose in Suffering 235

Day 5: Unshakable Joy: Finding Your Strength in God's Purpose 239

Day 6: Your Unfolding Story: A Life Lived for His Kingdom 243

Day 7: Road to Purpose: Your Kingdom Destiny Awaits 247

Conclusion 251

About the Author 255

AUTHOR'S NOTE

Hi friend! My name is Monika Harrison, and I am a primary school teacher who has dedicated many years to nurturing, loving, and caring for young hearts and minds, helping them discover the joy of learning and the wonder and beauty of the world around them. Now, I am thrilled to share a different kind of lesson—one that springs from my deepest convictions and personal walk with Christ. This book, *The Providential Road to Purpose*, marks my first venture into nonfiction Christian writing, a journey I have embarked on with immense prayer and passion. My hope and desire is to offer encouragement, insight, and a fresh perspective on faith that resonates with everyday life. Just as I strive and plan to make complex ideas accessible to my students, I aim to present spiritual truths in a clear, relatable, and inspiring way.

It is my hope and passion that through these pages, readers like you will find moments of reflection, renewed hope, and a deeper and more intimate connection with God. Whether you are a seasoned believer or just beginning to explore your faith, my prayer is that *The Providential Road to Purpose* will be a source of comfort, challenge, and abiding joy.

When not in the classroom or writing, I can be found running to my favorite worship music, enjoying quiet mornings with a cup of coffee and my Bible, or spending time with my family. I live in sunny Florida with my wonderful husband and two beautiful children.

Thank you for joining me on this journey. May God bless you richly as you seek Him.

HOW TO PILGRIMAGE THROUGH THIS BOOK

Dear Reader,

This book is a message of hope for living missionally for the kingdom of God. It is a journey of faith. There are many stories interlaid in each chapter that are inspired and drawn from my own life. We will journey together through this book. I will give you tools at the end of each chapter to help you deepen your understanding of God's truth, apply those truths to your own life, and offer prayer and reflection to go deeper in relationship with God. We will call this section "Making It About Me", the 3 M's of your daily devotion:

Message: You will be given the message point from the chapter to reflect on and strengthen your focus for the day.

Missional: You will be provided reflection questions that will help you ponder and draw conclusions from your own journey and how to live missionally for God.

Meditate: I will lead you into a simple prayer on the teaching and the precepts for the day.

This is a book that gives you daily encouragement as you journey through life. I wrote this book as a friend sitting with you over a cup of coffee and chatting about how God is working in and through you to make you more like Him, transforming you and giving you the power to pursue your destiny to live on mission for His kingdom purposes. I have prayed and asked the Lord for wisdom and guidance as I wrote each day. Each chapter is a part of my own journey of faith. I know as you read and spend time reflecting on each daily devotion, you will be encouraged as I was to walk deeper with the Lord and pursue a life lived with purpose that brings glory to God, a life rooted in love and on mission for the kingdom of God.

INTRODUCTION

Hi, friend! I am overjoyed that you are here. I have been waiting to talk to you. I hope you have the time to sit back and enjoy a cup of your favorite warm beverage and kick your feet up, relax, and soak up a bit of encouragement as you journey through this book with me. I am a faith-filled encourager of HOPE (Heavenly Opportunities Prepared Eternal). I want to help you live a life filled with joy and purpose. I want you to know who you are and why you were created. I want you to have a life rooted in love. A life lived with passion and purpose.

This book is designed to be a simple and strategic read, giving you tools to deepen your understanding of Scripture and allowing the Holy Spirit to apply His teaching to help you live out your God-given purposes. This book reads like a devotional, with practical application to help you go deeper in relationship with God. It is reflective and meditative on biblical truths and how to apply these precepts to your life, transforming you to live on mission for God. Each chapter will uplift and encourage you to keep focused on a kingdom mindset and continue reaping a harvest, even when life and circumstances get hard and you want to give up. The tools at the end of each chapter will encourage and allow you to go deeper in relationship with God. This book was inspired by my favorite Scripture and the reason I do what I do, Galatians 6:9:

> Let us not become weary in doing good, for at the proper time we will reap a harvest if we do not give up.

Let's be honest and real transparent. Life is hard. There is no easy way around it. We have moments of complete joy and moments of pain and unfortunately, suffering. We can't predict life, but we can live in such a way that we can bring hope in every situation and help those around us as we navigate through our journey here on earth. A journey that is blessed by every peak and every valley. My hope for you and me is to be a blessing to the world around us. To the people we share life with and to those we don't. Even our enemies. (See James 1:2–8.)

I have had the privilege to walk through many trials in my life that refined who I am. Each trial shaped me into the woman I am today (1 Peter 1:3–7). I am a teacher, and I always share one of my favorite books with the women I encourage in my life, called *How Santa Got His Job* by Stephen Krensky. This book is about all the jobs Santa had to do before becoming who he was created to be—Santa. He was a toy maker, a mail carrier, a baker, a chimney sweeper, and a man in a circus flying out of a cannon. Each time, something unforeseen would happen that prepared him for the next job, which ultimately led him to his purpose in life. He was created to bless others and was being prepared to be Santa.

You also have a skill or job that prepares you for your destiny. Your treasures, gifts, and talents are given to you for a purpose. God works behind the scenes to prepare you for His will for your life. It's called Providence. His provisions lead you to your calling. A higher and more effective way to utilize your talents and treasures is serving and blessing others. This is a life lived abundantly with power in your purpose. I learned this through walking with the Lord through the disciplines of the faith, leading me to a deeper relationship with Him and His purposes for me.

Jesus is why I love, laugh, and live the way I do. He changed how I see myself and how I see you. You are not a stranger; you are a friend. We have gifts, treasures, and talents God has prepared for us in advance to live on mission for the kingdom of God. Each talent we have can be used for the purpose of blessing someone. I want you to know you are special. There is no one like you. God created you to be you (Ps. 139).

You are loved. You are beautiful. You are worthy. You are chosen. You are a child of God. You are seen, and you are His. If you are still reading this, then you probably are wondering how you know me and why you should care. You don't know the things that stir my heart. You don't know what I am going through or my thoughts and dreams. Well, I know who holds the answer to all these questions and more. His name is Jesus. He died to know you. He knows every hair on your head. He knows you intimately. He sees you, all of you, the broken parts, the messy parts, and He wants you to know He is with you. He sent me to love and encourage you to never give up. He is with you, and He will never leave you. He will never forsake you. He is a promise keeper. I pray you find encouragement and comfort here as you journey with me through the pages of this book. Do you know the one who holds all things together for our good and His glory? It is Jesus! Jesus is our connection. Jesus is the reason I get up every day. He is my strength and hope in every circumstance. Jesus is why I am sharing and encouraging you today and always. Jesus is why I love, laugh, and live the way I do. He changed how I see myself and how I see you. You are not a stranger; you are a friend.

We have more in common than you think. We are women (and men who may be reading this) living a life with many of the same hopes and dreams. We are women who walk in freedom and are rooted in love. We are women living a life that is lived with purpose. A life on mission for the kingdom of God. You are on the providential road to your purpose and kingdom destiny.

We all have a divine calling and a desire to pursue it. The key is unlocking your potential and your passions that will ultimately lead you to your kingdom purpose. I believe these seven principles will lead you to your kingdom destiny—a life lived with passion and perseverance to bring heaven here on earth in your everyday life. Living for the kingdom of God brings power to your purpose and a fulfilled life. The life you are meant to live. A transformed life lived for the kingdom of God.

I was talking to God one evening, asking for clarity on how I can teach others about how to live missionally, bringing heaven here on earth in our day-to-day interactions with each other, and how we can live our lives centered on kingdom purposes, bringing glory to God and deepening our relationship with Him. I started writing and praying through the process and formulated seven practical precepts that will transform your life, driving you to your kingdom destiny.

1. **Awareness**—Knowing who God is, who you are, and why you were created.

2. **Agreement**—God's call to live life righteously by walking in God's promises.

3. **Ability**—Living an obedient life engaging in the disciplines of the faith.

4. **Abandonment**—Surrendering your life and deepening your relationship with God.

5. **Adoration**—Living your life captivated by Jesus and loving others from a thankful heart.

6. **Action**—Living out the promises of God and trusting Jesus as you participate in His story.

7. **Aim**—Living a life transformed by God, driving you to live out your kingdom destiny.

This book is designed to be a practical tool that will encourage and guide you on your journey of faith. Each week I will discuss each precept in detail and how to apply it to your daily life. You will have seven days of devotion and reflection in areas that will help you draw closer to God through biblical truths and prayer.

Do you ever feel like you're working hard and doing all the right things, yet you still struggle to understand why circumstances or the visions you have for your future are standing still? Why the situation or things you are working on and putting all your effort into are not moving in the direction you hoped and prayed for? Why is it so hard in the waiting with God? I completed this book and began praying for clarity and direction as I embarked on taking this message to you, the reader. I was waiting and trusting the Lord for direction. I was drawing near to the Lord for deep soul nourishment after being in a car accident and feeling a bit anxious about driving.

I had a Scripture illuminate off the page while listening to a sermon, and it felt like the Lord was speaking into my current circumstance. Psalm 77:10–11 is a psalm of lament written by King David. It hit me like a wave and reminded me of all the Lord has brought me through over my life. It says, "Then I thought, 'To this I will appeal: the years when the Most High stretched out his right hand. I will remember the deeds of the LORD; yes, I will remember your miracles of long ago.'" I sat and reflected on God's provisions and promises of long ago, such as in the time of the prophet Moses, and how the promised land seemed so far out of reach for the Israelites. They struggled in the waiting. There was a time when they were so desperate they wanted to go back to enemy territory in Egypt. They did not see how they could escape when they were surrounded by their enemies. They stood at the water's edge of the Red Sea with no hope of crossing to the other side. They were stuck and needed divine intervention for help, but instead they struggled and cried out to God, expressing their regret at leaving Egypt and that they would have rather remained slaves. They let fear get in the way of their faith.

Do you ever feel that way in your life? Those times when circumstances seem hopeless and fear starts creeping in, reminding you of your Egypt? I know I do, and it takes a refocus and a positive mind shift to stop the thought from going in the wrong direction. A thought can lead you to destructive patterns, or it can lead you to your kingdom destiny and purpose. The lies of the enemy can shout into our insecurities, silencing the still, small voice of God. Shouting louder and louder to distract us from what God has planned ahead for us in our future. It is a trap. It can leave you stuck and often paralyzed in fear.

Our own emotions and will can stop us from seeing and believing the truth set before us. Don't let fear stop you from what lies ahead. Do it afraid. Keep moving forward even when it's hard. Even when it doesn't make sense. Even when it goes against everything that feels right. Do not look at the waters that seem to be raging all around you. Keep your eyes off the storm and on Jesus. God is faithful, and His unseen hand is working behind the scenes and will part your waters. Psalm 77:19–20 says, "Your path led through the sea, your way through the mighty waters, though your footprints were not seen. You led your people like a flock by the hand of Moses and Aaron." God is shepherding His flock even when things seem to be hopeless. He will part your Red Sea in His timing. There is a purpose in the waiting.

I later asked God for confirmation on what I was praying about while meditating on this Scripture for about a week. I was praying for my waters to part. My faith was getting stronger in this area of my life. I remember sitting down to listen to a sermon from a well-known pastor who had been on summer vacation for a few weeks. I was looking forward to his return all summer. He was doing a series titled "I Thought So." His first Scripture was Psalm 77! I thought to myself, *What are the odds that this Scripture I have been hyper-focused on would be an entire sermon I can learn from and go deeper?* I prayed and studied and was encouraged. I felt the weight of a burden slowly lift off as I studied this psalm. I prayed one morning as I was running, specifically for confirmation on this Scripture and what I was praying to be lifted. I wondered, *Was this the hand of God upon me?* I then prayed and asked for a third confirmation.

A week went by, and I completely forgot about it. I was at my weekly coffee night with a group of ladies. A friend stayed a little longer, and we were able to catch up on our summers. I told her about the things I was praying for and the psalm the Lord laid on my heart. She went home that night and was reading a Christian novel. She read a paragraph that spoke right into my situation, and the only Scripture that was mentioned thus far in the book was Psalm 77. She texted me the next morning. I told her she was my third confirmation. I do not believe in coincidences. That, my friend, was the Holy Spirit confirming and speaking right to my spirit. The Lord is good, all the time. All the time, the Lord is good, even in the waiting. We can allow our waiting time to be filled with anxiety and fear. We can sit in our misery or discomfort and try to make sense of it all, or we can choose faith. We can trust in the Lord's unfailing love for us. We can praise Him through it all. He is listening, and He will work it all out for your good and His glory. Psalm 13:5–6 shouts, "But I trust in your unfailing love; my heart rejoices in your salvation. I will sing the LORD's praise, for he has been good to me." I pray you sing through the fear, praise God, and shout through the waiting. Trust in His plans for you. They are always good. His unseen hand is carrying you to your kingdom purpose. I pray this book encourages and inspires you to walk closer with Jesus and empowers you to live on mission for the kingdom of God.

AWARENESS

AWARENESS—KNOWING WHO GOD IS, WHO YOU ARE, AND WHY YOU WERE CREATED.

And to put on the new self, created to be like
God in true righteousness and holiness.

EPHESIANS 4:24

John Calvin wrote, "Without knowledge of self, there is no knowledge of God." The definition of self-awareness with a biblical view is the ability to understand oneself, including personality, emotions, strengths, weaknesses, and sin tendencies, in light of God's truth. Self-awareness can help you understand how your actions impact yourself and others, enabling you to develop a kingdom mindset by learning from your mistakes, managing your emotions, and aligning your behavior with your beliefs. If your beliefs and actions are not aligned with God's, you are not living with a biblical worldview. The truth must align with your actions and your will in order to be living in the will of God, leading you to your purpose and destiny for the kingdom of God.

God is the creator and sustainer of all things. Romans 8:28 tells us, "And we know that in all things God works for the good of those who love him, who have been called according to his purpose." You have a purpose only you can fulfill as a child of God. You are called to use your time, treasures, and talents for kingdom purposes, leading you to a life that glorifies God and brings lasting contentment in all you do. When you put your trust in Jesus, you were adopted into the family of God. You are a chosen child and are seated with God in the heavenly realms (Eph. 2:6–7). You are positioned in Christ, and you are given heavenly privileges. As a child of God you are accepted, secure, and safe in God's kingdom. Trust in those promises and live like you are a daughter of a king, because you are! You have been adopted as a coheir in the kingdom. You are predestined to do good works that God prepared in advance for you to do (Eph. 2:10). Your story is being written as long as there is breath in your lungs. Your purpose is to love God and make Him known through your actions and words, glorifying God in all you do. You have a unique purpose that is being woven in God's providences in your life. Unlocking your purpose and kingdom destiny begins with self-awareness.

Let's take a journey together over the next week and discover how God has uniquely designed you to unlock your kingdom purpose through *Awareness*.

THE GOODNESS OF GOD: EVEN WHEN LIFE IS HARD

I want to encourage you today to continue trusting and leaning into God, even if it still hurts. Even if you want to give up. Even if your prayers have not been answered yet. He is a *good* God. He sees you, and He is working through you. He is not against you. He delights in you. He wants the best for you. God knows what you are going through. He sees your struggles. Take refuge in Him. His love endures forever, and He is faithful. Trust in Him today. I hear the same questions from so many women who struggle with their faith: Why would a good God let bad things happen? Where is God in this? How can God be good if He allows evil to be in this world? Why are my prayers not being answered? If God is good, why doesn't He answer my prayers the way I want them answered? Doesn't He want me to be happy? He loves me, right? I do all the right things, and still God lets this happen. Is God even listening to me? Honestly, we all have had these questions along our walk with the Lord. Some of these questions we can't answer this side of heaven, but we surely can look at what we do know.

I know that God created the heavens and the earth in the beginning, and He said it was good in Genesis 1:31. I also know we live in a fallen world and that bad things happen all the time due to sin entering our story through Adam and Eve. When things happen to us or around us that seem difficult or even unbearable, it is the result of the fall (Gen. 3). God allows these things to happen, but He is a good and faithful God. I am reminded of Genesis

50:20 (ESV): "As for you, you meant evil against me, but God meant it for good, to bring it about that many people should be kept alive, as they are today." This verse reveals God's authority and His remarkable ability to orchestrate events, even those driven by malice, to ultimately serve His good purposes.

God will work it out, but His timing is sometimes not aligned with ours. His timing is perfect. Trust. God's goodness is not based on our feelings in a situation or a seasonal circumstance. Psalm 34:8 states, "Taste and see that the LORD is good; blessed is the one who takes refuge in him." It's a call to actively seek and perceive God's goodness through living and connecting with Him. Psalm 100:5 (ESV) says, "For the LORD is good; his steadfast love endures forever, and his faithfulness to all generations." This confirms God's fundamental goodness and loving character. Spending time in the presence of God will deepen your faith. You will see His will working in your life and His goodness that never fades, despite your circumstances. Living out His promises and connecting in deep intimacy with the Lord will bring lasting connection.

First Corinthians 1:9 (ESV) says, "God is faithful, by whom you were called into fellowship with his Son, Jesus Christ our Lord." This verse underscores God's dedication to fulfilling what He has promised. Furthermore, 2 Timothy 2:13 says, "If we are faithless, he remains faithful, for he cannot disown himself." Even when people are unfaithful, God's commitment remains steadfast because His unchanging nature and dedication to His promises ("he cannot disown himself") assure believers of His continued faithfulness, even amid their doubts or failures.

I remember a time I was angry with God due to losing my mom to cancer and my dad to heart failure in my twenties. My faith was wavering in that season of my life, which led me to make many bad choices and drew me further from God. It led me into temptation and ultimately sinful behavior. I still believed in God, but so does the devil. I stopped praying and let my anger and grief guide my decisions. I lacked connection and intimacy with God, which caused my heart to harden and stirred me toward many things that did not sustain or satisfy my longing for connection to something greater than myself. My faith had no object. It was blind faith. The journey was long, but God pursued me and led me back to Him through a series of trials and tribulations. My faith was refined through fire. There were many beautiful moments along the way. I have a wonderful husband and two beautiful children and a life lived abundantly in Christ. God blessed me tenfold in my life. My faith is no longer blinded by my pain. My faith object is Jesus. He is faithful, and He is good to me all the time, even in the muck and the mire. I have learned to trust in Him with my whole heart and surrender to His will.

God will redeem all things. Revelation 21:5 says, "He who was seated on the throne said, 'I am making everything new!' Then he said, 'Write this down, for these words are trustworthy and true.'" This verse is filled with hope and the assurance that God will ultimately correct all wrongs and usher in a completely new reality. The beauty in this broken world is the gift of Jesus. God came in the flesh and entered our story. He died a death we deserved. He was our sacrifice and atonement for sin—a spotless lamb.

Jesus came to bring life and redemption to all who believe in Him. It is a free gift to all. The Father's goodness and faithfulness to us is His Son's death on the cross. The redemptive work was in the resurrection when God the Father raised Jesus to life. The power is the Holy Spirit given to dwell within us as children of God.

I pray you lean into Jesus today. He is your strength and your salvation. God is good, all the time. All the time, God is good.

MAKING IT ABOUT ME

Message: *God is faithful to us and works everything out for our good and His glory, according to His kingdom purposes.* Read the following Scriptures and meditate on these truths for a while. Let them simmer in your spirit before moving on.

> 1 Corinthians 1:9 (ESV): "God is faithful, by whom you were called into the fellowship of his Son, Jesus Christ our Lord."

2 Timothy 2:13: "If we are faithless, he remains faithful, for he cannot disown himself."

Genesis 50:20 (ESV): "As for you, you meant evil against me, but God meant it for good, to bring it about that many people should be kept alive, as they are today."

Missional: Take a few moments and write down what God's faithfulness has looked like over your life. What has been your faith object? Are you living like you serve a good God?

Meditate: I pray you lean into Jesus today. He is your strength and your salvation. God is good, all the time. All the time, God is good. Take a few moments and spend time with God. I will lead you in a prayer.

Heavenly Father,

Thank You for loving me first. I lean on You for my strength and my salvation. You are working everything out for my good and Your glory. Keep my eyes fixed on You, the author and perfecter of my faith. Jesus, You are my faith object now and forever.

In the holy name of Jesus, Amen

THE BATTLE FOR YOUR MIND: FINDING FREEDOM IN CHRIST

I want to encourage you today to see yourself the way God sees you—the real you. You are uniquely created for a purpose only you can fulfill. You have power in your purpose and your position in Christ.

If I asked you to tell me about yourself, what would you say? What do you identify yourself with? How would you describe yourself to me? What defines you? Are you living a life basing your identity on what the culture tells you? What makes *you*? Would you identify yourself by your profession, your hobbies, your sexuality, your socioeconomic status, or your physical attributes? Most of us, when asked the question, "Who are you?" would talk about our profession, our hobbies, and whether or not we are married with children. It's the typical answer, the easiest way to define us. But what if I asked you to tell me about yourself without giving me physical attributes or worldly cultural identities? Could you tell me who you really are? How do you see yourself? Do you see yourself the way others see or define you? How do you see yourself in God's eyes? How do you see God?

Recognizing your self-worth and self-awareness leads you to a deeper understanding of your identity and your position in Christ. According to 2 Peter 1:5–7, faith is just the starting point. We are called to diligently develop virtue, knowledge, self-control, endurance, godliness, brotherly kindness, and love, which will deepen our self-awareness and our relationship with God. It is vital to understand truth so you are not deceived by the lies of this world, which are driven by darkness.

Three times Jesus referred to Satan as "the ruler of this world" (John 12:31; 14:30; 16:11). Other passages of Scripture call Satan "the god of this world" (2 Cor. 4:4) and "the prince of the power of the air" (Eph. 2:2), informing us "that the whole world lies in the power of the evil one" (1 John 5:19). If you are a child of God and have put your trust in Him, you have authority and power over the enemy in the name of Jesus.

You are positioned in Christ, seated in heavenly places with Him. Your position in Christ refers to the spiritual standing and core identity of someone who believes, emphasizing your union with Jesus Christ, a union that results in your being seen as sharing His heavenly seat and being blessed with a complete array of spiritual gifts. You have power in your position with Christ. Your identity is no longer tied to self but to your union with Christ. You are in Christ and no longer part of this world but an heir to the kingdom of God. Colossians 3:1–2 (ESV) tells us: "If then you have been raised with Christ, seek the things that are above, where Christ is seated at the right hand of God. Set your minds on things that are above, not on things that are on earth." You need to train your mind to focus on spiritual realities and eternal purposes because you died to your old self; your true life is now secure with Christ in God. "When Christ who is your life appears, then you also will appear with him in glory" (v. 4). The more you know and understand the promises of God, the more you will recognize the lies of the enemy. In 2 Corinthians 10:5, Paul writes, "We demolish arguments and every pretension that sets itself up against the knowledge of God, and we take captive every thought to make it obedient to Christ."

I have struggled with nightmares since I was a little girl. I had episodes of sleep paralysis later in life. I would wake up from very intense demonic dreams. These intensified as I was drawing nearer and deeper in my walk with Christ. I was going to church regularly and practicing some of the disciplines of the faith. I had faith and belief, but I still struggled with patterns of sin and could not pray the battle in my mind away. It started to affect me physically and emotionally. I remember struggling to fall asleep at night; I felt heaviness like a weight on my chest. It was like I was in a tunnel, and I could not seem to shake this feeling off.

I was at church one Sunday, and during baptisms, I felt a strong urge in my spirit to seek out help. It was not like me to talk about my feelings, let alone tell someone I barely knew what I was experiencing, for fear of being judged or thought of as crazy. I walked out of service, and my pastor was right in front of me. To this day I am thankful for the direction to a biblical counselor to walk me through the steps to freedom in Christ—a pivotal moment in my life. I was in a spiritual battle, a battle of my mind. I was ignorant of my position in Christ. After I prayed out loud and repented of all my sins, the weight and heaviness lifted. I remember carrying "I am" statements of being a child of God in my purse and repeating them to myself daily. I would pray out loud before I went to sleep and would continually pray the Word of God over myself and my family. The dreams still happen on occasion, but now I am in battle over the demonic force in my dream. I rebuke it with my authority in Christ. I no longer fear it. I stand firm in Christ.

I no longer identify myself with my sin. I see myself through the eyes of Christ. I am reminded of Psalm 139:13–14 (GW): "You alone created my inner being. You knitted me together inside my mother. I will give thanks to you because I have been so amazingly and miraculously made. Your works are miraculous, and my soul is fully aware of this." My soul magnifies the Lord and is no longer enslaved to sin. There is no condemnation in Christ Jesus. I am free! Free indeed!

You are a child of God, chosen and deeply loved by your Father in heaven. He created you for a purpose that He planned for you to do. Your purpose and destiny can only be brought to completion by God. How do you access this knowledge and wisdom, and how do you start living your life with a kingdom mindset, bringing your purpose to completion? You must have an understanding and knowledge of who God is and what He has done for you, turn from the desires of the flesh, and have a reverent fear of Him.

I pray that you stand firm against the enemy's schemes. You have power and authority as a child of God. You are His.

MAKING IT ABOUT ME

Message: *You are a child of God, chosen and deeply loved by your Father in heaven. You are uniquely created for a purpose only you can fulfill. You have power in your purpose and your position in Christ.* Read the following Scriptures and meditate on these truths for a while. Let them simmer in your spirit before moving on.

> 2 Peter 1:5–7: "For this very reason, make every effort to add to your faith goodness; and to goodness, knowledge; and to knowledge, self-control; and to self-control, perseverance; and to perseverance, godliness; and to godliness, mutual affection; and to mutual affection, love."

> Colossians 3:1–2 (ESV): "If then you have been raised with Christ, seek the things that are above, where Christ is, seated at the right hand of God. Set your minds on things that are above, not on things that are on earth."

> Psalm 139:13–14 (GW): "You alone created my inner being. You knitted me together inside my mother. I will give thanks to you because I have been so amazingly and miraculously made. Your works are miraculous, and my soul is fully aware of this."

Missional: Take a few moments and write down: How would you describe the way you see God? How does God see you? Write three things that identify you as a child of God.

Meditate: I pray that you stand firm against the enemy's schemes. You have power and authority in your position in Christ. You are His. You are accepted, safe, and secure as a child of God.

Heavenly Father,

Thank You for knitting me together in my mother's womb. I am fearfully and wonderfully made. You have chosen me as Your child, seating me in the heavenly realms. Keep my eyes on the things above. Help me turn from the desires of my flesh and have a reverent fear of You, Lord. Standing firm in my faith. You are my refuge and my strength.

In Jesus's mighty name, Amen

FROM BURDEN TO BLESSING: THE PATH TO SPIRITUAL REST

I want to encourage you today to lay your burdens at the feet of Jesus. He will give you rest for your soul.

Are you truly living your best life? Or does striving for more leave you feeling utterly empty? Does the world appear shattered and hopeless? Are you overwhelmed by anxiety and helplessness, desperately seeking peace yet unable to find it, even in serene settings?

These are some of the questions I have struggled with in my life. I believe we are created by God to search and seek for something more than ourselves or the objects of our deepest desires. We are always longing for hope, for peace, and for a deeper love than we can grasp in others. Yes, we can love others and find comfort and peace in moments with them, but even those relationships can and will fail us. We cannot and should not put all our hope in an object of our affection. It will not satisfy or complete us, leaving us feeling empty, unfulfilled, and striving for something or someone else to fill the void. That void longs to be satisfied and sustained with lasting relief. How do we fill such a space within us that is wanting something or someone more? How can we maintain calm amid the demands of daily life?

I remember a time when I was surrounded by so much angst, grief, and utter doom due to my circumstances. There seemed to be no end in sight; it was one struggle after another. Can you relate? I could not seem to find solace and rest in anything. I would lie awake at night with no peace of mind. One night, I was completely vulnerable with the Lord. I came to Jesus with child-like faith and an absolute surrender of will. I prayed for a deeper presence with Him and an answer to much of my life's and the world's brokenness. The Lord gave me peace in that moment I will never forget—His presence. The Lord took my burdens away and gave me His peace, a gift I will cherish until I meet Jesus face-to-face.

Matthew 11:28 says: "Come to me, all you who are weary and burdened, and I will give you rest."

True rest, as Jesus offers, is a state of spiritual peace and comfort, a refuge in His presence, not just physical relief. It's a deep, soul-level rest, a peace that surpasses physical weariness, which Jesus makes available.

Jesus further states in Matthew 11:30, "For my yoke is easy and my burden is light." Jesus offers spiritual peace and tranquility to those who seek His guidance and teachings.

I still have moments that can be overwhelming, and I still have trials that bring pain and suffering. But I now have that inner peace and calm only the Holy Spirit can bring amid the chaos.

Cast all your cares onto Jesus (1 Peter 5:7). He wants to know you and help you. Come to Him today.

MAKING IT ABOUT ME

Message: *Cast your burdens on Jesus, and He will give you rest for your weary soul.* Read the following Scriptures and meditate on these truths for a while. Let them simmer in your spirit before moving on.

> Matthew 11:28: "Come to me, all you who are weary and bur-dened, and I will give you rest."
>
> Matthew 11:30: "For my yoke is easy and my burden is light."
>
> 1 Peter 5:7: "Cast all your anxiety on him because he cares for you."

Missional: Take a few moments and write down a time of day when you can connect with God. Be consistent and set apart at least fifteen minutes or more of your day to spend time with the Lord. Ask yourself: What area of my life is leaving me weary? What do I need to lay down at the feet of Jesus today?

Meditate: I pray for your well-being. I pray you let go and give all your burdens to Jesus. No burden is too heavy for Him. I pray you lean into Jesus and find rest for your weary soul. He loves you and wants you to come to Him and release all your burdens unto Him today. His promises are good. If you follow His ways, He will lead you out of darkness into His marvelous light (1 Peter 2:9).

Heavenly Father,

Thank You for Your enduring love for me. I come to You, Lord, with all my burdens. I lay them at Your feet. I trust in Your sovereignty and goodness over my life. I cast every care onto You because You care for me. You tell me in Your Word that Your yoke is easy, and Your burden is light. I release all my burdens to You now.

In Jesus's mighty name, Amen

TAKE UP YOUR CROSS: A CALL TO FAITH

I want to encourage you today to take up your cross and walk by faith.

Are you experiencing a life driven by faith? Is your faith bigger than the daily mountains you face?

What does it truly mean to take up your cross daily? Why do we have a cross to bear when Jesus paid our debt in full on the cross for us? These are questions I have asked on my journey of faith. I am learning to pick up my cross differently as I walk out my faith.

As a kindergarten teacher, I find that teaching a skill and modeling it are ways students learn, but when a student starts to do a hands-on activity with that same lesson and struggles, there is opportunity for growth. When I guide the student through the lesson as they navigate the difficult content and succeed, the lesson starts to make sense, and the student gains a better understanding and knowledge.

Learning by doing seems to have a lasting effect on the learner. I wonder if God teaches us this way. We must experience the hard circumstances to understand the lesson being taught. It draws us closer to Jesus, we learn far more, and our faith is deepened. Taking up our cross daily is a sacrifice and a surrender to self.

Matthew 16:24–25 says: "Then Jesus said to his disciples, 'Whoever wants to be my disciple must deny themselves and take up their cross and follow me. For whoever wants to save their life will lose it, but whoever loses their life for me will find it.'"

Following Jesus requires complete self-denial and a willingness to sacrifice everything, even one's own desires. Jesus asks His followers to prioritize Him above all else, embracing hardship and putting their own needs last. We bear our cross daily because of the love Jesus displayed on that wooden cross. We surrender all to Jesus because He loved us first.

Galatians 2:20 says: "I have been crucified with Christ and I no longer live, but Christ lives in me. The life I now live in the body, I live by faith in the Son of God, who loved me and gave himself for me."

This verse speaks of a radical surrender to God, where one's own will and desires are set aside to live according to God's will. This is a choice we must make every day: to surrender our desires for His desires, to sacrifice our comforts, and to embrace selflessness to make a radical difference in the lives around us. A surrendered life is a life lived abundantly and for a greater purpose.

A few months ago, I was struggling with my classroom. I was finding it difficult to let the frustration go. I was getting overwhelmed and began questioning, *Is this for me?* Now I know the answer to this, but it doesn't make the difficult seasons any easier. I know the classroom is where the Lord has me. Many years ago the Lord laid on my heart that I was His ambassador in school. I didn't realize at the time the meaning and depth of that cross I would bear. I love what I do, but there are days when you just want to give up. This particular day was one of them. I remember feeling a bit overwhelmed as a child was having a tantrum, and I remember praising the Lord because I was able to have inner peace as the chaos surrounded me.

The next morning, I was cleaning the table before school, and a little cross charm popped into my hand out of nowhere. The first thought that came to my mind was, *Monika, take up your cross daily*. I knew right away this was the Lord speaking to my heart. I felt that nudge that everything would be okay. Later that afternoon, I received further confirmation that this was from the Lord. I was at my afternoon duty when my custodian came in and told me there was something in the bathroom and I needed to come check it out. I went to my room, and there, all over the bathroom walls, were crosses written in crayon. I remember the three crosses next to each other. I don't know who put them there, but I did know I was meant to see them. I felt a sense of peace come over me. I knew that I was not alone, and the Lord is with me, and I can bear my burdens with Him. I surrender my will every day and sacrifice for the good of others. The Lord shines in and through me. I will gladly take up my cross daily if it brings glory to Him.

MAKING IT ABOUT ME

Message: *Take up your cross daily and live by faith.* Read the following Scriptures and meditate on these truths for a while. Let them simmer in your spirit before moving on.

> Matthew 16:24–25: "Then Jesus said to his disciples, 'Whoever wants to be my disciple must deny themselves and take up their cross and follow me. For whoever wants to save their life will lose it, but whoever loses their life for me will find it.'"

> Galatians 2:20: "I have been crucified with Christ and I no longer live, but Christ lives in me. The life I now live in the body, I live by faith in the Son of God, who loved me and gave himself for me."

Missional: Take a few moments and write down the area of your life you know you need to surrender to God. What are some things in this world we chase after, and how might they pose a threat to our souls? How can we as Christians be working to obey and walk in the fullness of discipleship? How can you take up your cross today?

Meditate: I pray you have the faith to take up *your* cross daily. Your cross is yours to bear. The Lord will give you what you need as you surrender and sacrifice your will to Him.

Heavenly Father,

Thank You for the sacrificial love You gave us in Your Son, Jesus. He died on a cross so that we may live. I surrender my life to Your will today. I take up my cross and follow You with all my heart. You are my rock and my salvation.

In the mighty name of Jesus, Amen

FORGIVE, FORGET, FIX: A GODLY STRATEGY

I want to encourage you today to forgive anyway. The Lord is in the details of your life. He knows, He sees, He cares. He will work in the heart of the person that hurt you.

Are you a forgiving person? Do you hold a grudge against another if they hurt you in some way? Do you immediately get defensive or justify your actions if you are wrong? Do you apologize when you know you are wrong or have hurt someone with your actions or words? Do you let pride get in the way of forgiveness?

Colossians 3:13 tells us: "Bear with each other and forgive one another if any of you has a grievance against someone. Forgive as the Lord forgave you." Bearing with others is about responding with understanding and kindness, even when they are frustrating or have wronged you.

Choosing to forgive is a process of letting go. It involves the active step of releasing bitterness and the desire for revenge. This is difficult for us to do when we have been hurt or wronged by another person, especially those in our inner circle. Forgiveness must come from our heart. It's not just the words we speak; it is a complete surrender of our pridefulness and will.

The Lord tells us in Matthew 18:21–22: "Then Peter came to Jesus and asked, 'Lord, how many times shall I forgive my brother or sister who sins against me? Up to seven times?' Jesus answered, 'I tell you, not seven times, but seventy-seven times.'"

Jesus emphasizes that forgiveness is an act of compassion and a sign of humility within God's kingdom. We forgive *even if*. We give our pain and burden to the Lord. He will work it out for our good. We let God handle the rest in the hearts of those that hurt us.

I am reminded of a strategy the Lord gave me many years ago in my classroom. I was redirecting a student's behavior, and he became very upset. He withdrew and started to become angry. I was not sure how to encourage or help him in that moment, so I asked the Lord to help me. The first thought that came to my mind was: *Forgive, Forget, Fix.*

I said to the student that I forgive him for what he is doing and I already forgot about it, but to please fix it so I don't have to revisit this with him again. It worked! Later, when I had time to reflect, I realized that this is exactly what Jesus does with us. He forgives us for our sin and forgets it as far as the east is from the west, and He tells us to repent and turn from our sin so He doesn't need to revisit this with us again. It is for our good. I still use this strategy today.

Forgive even when the person did not apologize. Forgiveness sets *your* heart free. Let God do the mending and disciplining in other people's hearts. You will see change in *you*.

MAKING IT ABOUT ME

Message: *Forgive as the Lord forgave you.* Read the following Scriptures and meditate on these truths for a while. Let them simmer in your spirit before moving on.

> Colossians 3:13: "Bear with each other and forgive one another if any of you has a grievance against someone. Forgive as the Lord forgave you."

> Matthew 18:21–22: "Then Peter came to Jesus and asked, 'Lord, how many times shall I forgive my brother or sister who sins against me? Up to seven times?' Jesus answered, 'I tell you, not seven times, but seventy-seven times.'

Missional: Take a few moments and reflect on what forgiveness looks like in your own life. How has God's forgiveness been experienced in your life? Is there anyone that you are struggling to forgive? What makes extending forgiveness in your situation difficult? How can forgiveness be practically expressed to someone who has wronged you?

Meditate: I pray you let go of the resentment and bitterness that has entangled you and forgive the other person and yourself and allow the Holy Spirit to work on both of your hearts. There is freedom when we forgive and give it to God.

Heavenly Father,

Thank You for Your forgiveness that has washed me white as snow. I am free from any condemnation, and I want to extend that forgiveness to others in my life. Help me let go of the hurt and pain that has a grip on me in this area of my life. I forgive those that have caused me pain. I give them to You, Lord.

In Jesus's name, Amen

DESTINED FOR DIVINE PURPOSE

I want to encourage you today to focus on the promises God has for you as His child. You are safe and secure in His arms, and He has a plan and a purpose for your life that is far greater than you could ever ask or imagine.

Are you living like you are worthy of your calling and purpose? Do you have a propensity to water down the life you are leading because you do not deem it worthy by the world's standards? Do you let others make you feel like you're less than what God has called you to be? Are you letting the world dictate your status quo? Do you view your life from God's perspective? Do you live your life for a higher purpose, or do you live your life to get to a future that you dreamed up in your mind? A security in a distant hope for peace and happiness that leaves you striving and spending all your energy now, leaving you drained physically and emotionally? Do you let your past dictate your future? Are you living the life God has planned for you?

Ephesians 2:10 tells us, "For we are God's handiwork, created in Christ Jesus to do good works, which God prepared in advance for us to do." God created us in His likeness, preparing us for living out our calling using our time, treasures, and talents to do what He prepared in advance for us to do. We are called to live a life of service, doing good and living on mission for the kingdom of God. Does your life reflect a desire for selfish gain, or a desire to give glory to God?

We each have a divine calling in our life. You have unique gifts that have been in you since you were a child. Those passions and desires are the things that bring you joy and are a part of His bigger plan for you. Unlocking those talents and treasures is the key to your divine calling and destiny. What desires or passions in your life can be used for kingdom purposes?

What areas of your life can you use to bring glory to God? God will bring your transformative life to fruition in His timing. We must be living in obedience and in His will in order to live out our divine calling. There is purpose in His provisions.

God prepares us on our journey, caring and protecting us as we navigate life. God works it all out, even if we stumble or get off our divine path. We sometimes must take detours, and that is okay because God's providence is leading us to our divine purpose.

I remember as a young child playing school with my stuffed animals. I loved learning and enjoyed pretending to be the teacher. I was a very shy child and was bullied a lot growing up because of my lazy eye. I felt much like an outcast to my peers. I eventually grew out of that shyness but never forgot the pain that others had caused me in my early years of school. I never would have dreamed that I was going to be a teacher and that God would bring redemption in my life and in so many others through my journey of teaching. I believe that through every experience I had growing up, God was preparing me for my calling.

I remember when I realized that school was where the Lord was using me as His ambassador. I didn't know the impact my life would have on others around me until I became a teacher. I have used this as a divine platform to bring the love of Jesus to those around me. I am living missionally for the kingdom of God. I bring glory to God in all I do, allowing the Holy Spirit to work in and through me—making me a vessel of love to those around me. You are living out your purpose when you are living missionally and serving the world around you, bringing all the glory to God.

MAKING IT ABOUT ME

Message: *Focus on the promises of God and His plans for you as His child.* Read the following Scripture and meditate on this truth for a while. Let it simmer in your spirit before moving on.

> Ephesians 2:10: "For we are God's handiwork, created in Christ
> Jesus to do good works, which God prepared in advance for us to do."

Missional: Take a few moments and reflect on your life and how God has been working behind the scenes bringing you to His perfect plan for your life. In what areas do you see God moving and working? How can you continue living missionally in those areas?

Meditate: I pray you continue to lean into God and allow the Holy Spirit to work in and through you, bringing redemption in every area of your life, leading you to your divine purpose: a life lived on mission for the kingdom of God.

Heavenly Father,

*Thank You for not leaving or forsaking me. You have a divine plan for
my life far greater than mine. I pray You give me clarity in the areas
that will lead me to my divine calling. I trust in the process. I am Your
handiwork, like clay in a potter's hands. Lord, mold me into the child
You created me to be. You deserve all power and glory forever and ever.*

In the mighty name of Jesus, Amen

LET GO, LET GOD: FINDING PEACE IN HIS PERFECT PLAN

I want to encourage you to let go of this world and the desires it brings and submit everything to the will of God. Allow the Holy Spirit to transform your life and bring fullness and redemption, making your path straight and helping you live the life you were always meant to live. Trust in His plan for you.

Do you find yourself looking for the next best thing? Using social media, television, or magazines to justify or compare your life to the lives around you? Do you get your self-worth and motivation from people in high places or those we deem important in our culture? Are you constantly trying to gratify your flesh with the things of this world? Is your flesh winning? Do you long for contentment and peace in the things you already have? What if I told you that you have everything you need right now, in this moment? Striving for more isn't going to bring you peace or happiness. It will leave you empty and continually wanting more. Let your striving cease, and focus on the things that bring contentment and lasting joy.

Matthew 6:33 says, "But seek first his kingdom and his righteousness, and all these things will be given to you as well." This verse inspires believers to seek God above all else and to live righteously, trusting that their needs will be provided. We must first seek the things that God desires for us. We have to surrender ourselves to the promises of God, allowing for spaces of healing and redemption in our lives. Trusting that the Lord's plans are higher and better than ours. Letting go of our desires and passions that don't align with God's.

The most important aspect of letting go is trust. You have to trust in the will of God. One of my favorite Scriptures is Proverbs 3:5–6: "Trust in the LORD with all your heart and lean not on your own understanding; in all your ways submit to him, and he will make your paths straight." This proverb encourages us to trust in God's wisdom and guidance rather than leaning on our own. Submitting to God with all our heart, letting go of our understanding, will begin a journey toward a divine path in life that is clear and aligned with God's plan.

I recently had to let go of my own stubborn will and let God move me in a different direction for His purposes. I had taught at an elementary school for twelve years and had built so many beautiful relationships over the years. God was with me in the trenches every step of the way during my journey teaching there. I thought I would retire at this school, but God had a different plan, and it took me a while to catch on.

About a year or so ago, I was praying and asking God to open the door for another opportunity. Every door that I tried to open remained closed. I distinctly remember hearing God tell me in my heart not to fear the closed doors. *You will clearly know when I am opening the door.* Looking back, I am thankful that door did not open because so many beautiful blessings occurred within those two years of teaching that only could have come from God. Lives were changed and redemption was made in those spaces.

I realized through a series of events that the Lord was closing the door at my current school. I knew it was the right timing, but my heart did not want to believe it. I had to take a huge leap of faith and decide to trust in God's plan no matter the cost. I trusted that God would open a door and I would know that this was His plan for me. In the process of waiting, I did not just sit and do nothing; I looked for other opportunities in teaching. I knew if the door closed like it had in the past, well, then this was not the path, and I would have clarity and move in a different direction. I prayed. I trusted. I praised in the waiting. I never gave up. I knew that God's will was going to be done in His timing. The Lord opened a new door for me, and it was very clear that He had a bigger plan for me. I look forward to the spaces and opportunities that await on my new adventure with God. His promises are good and His timing is perfect. The mission continues.

MAKING IT ABOUT ME

Message: *Let go and let God direct your path.* Read the following Scriptures and meditate on these truths for a while. Let them simmer in your spirit before moving on.

> Matthew 6:33: "But seek first his kingdom and his righteousness, and all these things will be given to you as well."
>
> Proverbs 3:5-6: "Trust in the LORD with all your heart and lean not on your own understanding; in all your ways submit to him, and he will make your paths straight."

Missional: Take a few moments and reflect on your life and the paths that may be crooked and need clarity and direction from God. What drives you in the morning and brings you peace? What areas of your life hinder your walk with God? List some areas of your life that you need to let go and give to God.

Meditate: I pray you let go and let God work everything out in your life. Submit to Him in every way, and you will see your paths in life become straight. You have to let go of the desires of the flesh and self, and let the Holy Spirit transform you into who you were always created to be. Trust.

Heavenly Father,

Thank You for the paths that brought me to You. Your providence has been my strength on my journey of faith. Help me seek the things of righteousness and goodness, bringing glory to You, Lord. I trust in You and all Your ways, and I know You will make my paths straight in Your perfect timing.

In Jesus's name, Amen

AGREEMENT

AGREEMENT—GOD'S CALL TO LIVE LIFE RIGHTEOUSLY BY WALKING IN GOD'S PROMISES.

*Praise the Lord. Blessed are those who fear the
Lord, who find great delight in his commands.*

PSALM 112:1

Obedience is acting in a constant state of righteousness. Living out God's promises and turning from our sinful desires and pursuing holiness. Charles Spurgeon said, "Obedience to the will of God is the pathway to perpetual honor and everlasting joy." When you obey God's commands and align your actions with God's will, you will have peace and fulfillment, leading you to joy and contentment in all you do. Walking by faith, living a life honoring to God, and trusting in the Lord's provision will bring lasting joy and contentment. Living a life that is pleasing to God aligns you with God's will and leads you to your calling in life. Let's spend time this week focusing on ways we can honor God with our obedience.

THE KEY TO GOD'S PROMISES: WALKING IN OBEDIENCE

I want to encourage you today to set your mind on things above and walk in God's promises. Be obedient to your call in life. You are His treasured possession.

Obedience is the key to unlocking the door to God's plan for your life. Leading a life that is honoring to God was our original design in the garden of Eden. God delights in our obedience and commands us to turn from our sin and follow His covenant.

Exodus 19:5 says, "Now if you obey me fully and keep my covenant, then out of all nations you will be my treasured possession." This verse establishes that through obedience God delights in us and we are treasured. This promise reveals not only God's love for His people but also His divine purpose for our lives.

Your identity is not your sin or sin pattern. You are defined by what Jesus did for you on the cross. Your identity is in Christ once you put your trust in Him. Stop letting your sin take hold of your life. Turn from it and keep your eyes on God's promises. God loves you, and nothing you do will change that once you are His child. The blood of Jesus washed you clean. The love of Jesus is unconditional toward you, but when you sin, it grieves the Holy Spirit and pushes you further away from God if you dwell there. Repent and turn from your fleshly desires and live like you are a child of the Most High. We all struggle with sin and can easily be prone to wander. We are imperfect people in a world trying to entice us and lead us down a crooked path. It is imperative as believers to create spaces to spend with the Lord, praying and allowing the Holy Spirit to guide and teach you as you journey through this life. Your love for Jesus is displayed in your obedience.

John 14:15 says, "If you love me, keep my commands." This Scripture reveals to us that our love for Jesus is reflected in our obedience to His commands. It's not a requirement to earn His love but an expression of the love we have for Him. Obedience is a natural result of following Jesus and His teachings.

I have believed in God since I was a child, but it was not until I repented of my sinful desires and ways that I started seeing deep change in my life. I started losing desires that had kept me in the bondage of sin for a long time. My desires started to be God's desires for my life. I wanted to go deeper and learn more about God's commands and His teachings. This led me on a journey of faith that still brings me such joy and contentment in all I do.

I often hear people say, "I believe in God," but can I tell you that the devil believes in God too? Do you follow Jesus and His commands? There is a difference between knowing and doing. James 1:22 says, "Do not merely listen to the word, and so deceive yourselves. Do what it says." This passage emphasizes the importance of integrating faith and action. We are deceiving ourselves if we are not applying God's promises to our lives.

You are called by God to walk in obedience and live life abundantly in Him. You are a child worthy of a divine calling. Live out God's promises, and you will find everlasting peace and joy.

MAKING IT ABOUT ME

Message: *Obedience is the key to unlocking the door to God's plan for your life.* Read the following Scriptures and meditate on these truths for a while. Let them simmer in your spirit before moving on.

> Exodus 19:5: "Now if you obey me fully and keep my covenant,
> then out of all nations you will be my treasured possession."

John 14:15: "If you love me, keep my commands."

James 1:22: "Do not merely listen to the word, and so deceive yourselves. Do what it says."

Missional: Take a few moments and reflect on how you are walking out obedience in your life. Are you giving God all your devotion? Are you holding back areas in your life that hinder you from living in obedience? Write down the things you struggle with that do not align with God's commands. Give this to God and repent and turn from these patterns. You will find peace and contentment in alignment with God's promises.

Meditate: I pray you draw near to God and turn from your sinful nature and allow the Holy Spirit to guide you and heal you from the inside out on your journey of faith, leading you to your divine calling.

Heavenly Father,

Thank You for loving me first and forgiving me for all my iniquities.
Help me, Lord, with my sinful nature; soften my heart toward
things that You delight in for me, Lord. Allow my actions and
words to align with Your truth. Teach and guide me in all things.
I love You, Lord, and want to bring glory to You in all I do.

In Jesus's name, Amen

REVERENT FEAR: THE FOUNDATION OF WISDOM AND CONTENTMENT

I want to encourage you to draw near to the Lord in reverent fear and awe and commit yourself to all His promises. His ways are higher, and they lead you to a life that honors Him while gaining lasting contentment and wisdom.

Do you ever feel like you lack wisdom in areas of your life? Do you seek others to help make decisions for you? Do you allow yourself or others to make decisions without bringing them to God first? Do you have an irreverent or a holy fear of the Lord? Before we can have godly wisdom, we must understand God's holiness and His character. A biblical definition of fear is the awe and reverence felt in the presence of God and a deep respect and obedience for the Lord. Fear is also an inherent response to the adversity of sin.

Proverbs 9:10 says, "The fear of the LORD is the beginning of wisdom." This verse demonstrates that true wisdom begins with a spiritual mindset and a deep respect for God's preeminence. Those who fear the Lord have a continual awareness of Him, a deep reverence for Him, and a sincere commitment to obey Him.

I have gained more knowledge over the years as I've spent my time listening to the Lord in my quiet time. Talking to God is a two-way conversation. Sometimes I would sit in silence and just wait upon the Lord in prayer, and I would not hear from God but would still have peace. Other times the

Lord would give me wisdom and clarity through the Word or through vessels used by Him to speak into my situation. God speaks to us in many ways, mainly through His Word. The more I read and studied His Word, the deeper I grew in my love for the Lord. My prayer life became less about my needs and more about my gratitude and thankfulness for the things in my life. I have gained more wisdom and clarity in my time spent with God. I am in awe of the Lord and enjoy spending time in His presence.

MAKING IT ABOUT ME

Message: *Reverent fear of the Lord brings wisdom.* Read the following Scripture and meditate on this truth for a while. Let it simmer in your spirit before moving on.

Proverbs 9:10: "The fear of the LORD is the beginning of wisdom."

Missional: Take a few moments and reflect on areas in your life where you need wisdom and discernment. Have you prayed and asked God for guidance? What specific "life skills" do you need to fulfill the call the Lord has on your life? In what areas of your life do you most need God's wisdom?

Meditate: I pray you spend time with the Lord listening to Him through His Word. I pray you gain a deeper understanding and knowledge of His ways and develop a reverent awe of God.

Heavenly Father,

Thank You for Your sovereignty and will over my life. I pray I continue to walk in Your commands. Help me in the areas I struggle with and lack wisdom in. Bring me clarity as I trust in Your promises throughout my life. You are my rock and my redeeming grace. I am in awe of You, Lord.

In Jesus's mighty name, Amen

FROM BONDAGE TO BLESSING: EMBRACING GOD'S TRUTH

I want to encourage you to walk out your faith. Cling to the good things that bring fruitfulness into your life. Let go of the things that create pathways to guilt and shame, leaving you empty and feeling hopeless. Eliminate the things that hinder you from walking in God's truth.

Do you have guilty pleasures that you hide or play down when confronted? Are you aware of your sin but struggle to let it go? Do you find yourself in a cyclical pattern of sinful behaviors you can't seem to break, no matter how hard you try? There are many sinful patterns that seem harmless because they are not the "big" ones we deem in our culture to be forbidden, like murder or infidelity. Oftentimes, we water down our sin and deem it harmless—things like gluttony, white lies, or gossip. Can I encourage you to view every sin as a big sin? If you don't address all of your sinful patterns, they will grow and lead you into bondage. Sin is like a virus that infects you; if you do not address and treat it, it will lead you down deadly paths. The remedy is to turn from it and repent. This means doing a 180 and heading in the opposite direction and walking in obedience.

I know this isn't easy, and it takes commitment and perseverance to do things in alignment with God's will. The apostle Paul struggled with the same things we do. Romans 7:15–17 says: "I do not understand what I do. For what I want to do I do not do, but what I hate I do. And if I do what I do not want to do, I agree that the law is good. As it is, it is no longer I myself who do it, but it is sin living in me."

Paul describes the inner struggle of the new, Spirit-led believer and the old, fleshly, sinful desires that we still often cling to and that bend us toward sin. There isn't a button you can press once you become a believer that stops every cyclical pattern in your life. It takes commitment and a life lived in relationship with Jesus. Psalm 103:3 (ESV) says, "who forgives all your iniquity, who heals all your diseases."

This verse speaks of both physical and spiritual healing. God will heal you from your past mistakes and offer you a fresh start. Praise God for forgiveness and healing in your life!

I was in bondage to sin for a good part of my adult life. The crazy part is that I didn't know it. I did not see my sin as sin at all. That was the problem. I was living for me and the world that entangled and enticed me every day. It had a grip on my soul. I believed in God, but it was a "cuddly" god I created that fit the world I was living in at the time. I believed that because my god loved me and I had faith in him, it was okay to dabble in things that gratified my flesh. I am grateful that the Lord did not leave me or forsake me (Heb. 13:5). He pursued me and led me back to Him, and I learned what it truly means to have faith in Jesus.

MAKING IT ABOUT ME

Message: *Walk out your faith in obedience, clinging to the goodness of God.* Read the following Scriptures and meditate on these truths for a while. Let them simmer in your spirit before moving on.

> Romans 7:15–17: "I do not understand what I do. For what I want to do I do not do, but what I hate I do. And if I do what I do not want to do, I agree that the law is good. As it is, it is no longer I myself who do it, but it is sin living in me."

Psalm 103:3 (esv): "who forgives all your iniquity, who heals all your diseases."

Missional: Take a few moments and reflect on areas of your life that hinder you from walking in faith. What sins do you struggle to break in your life? What is one area of disobedience you can commit to the Lord today?

Meditate: I pray you draw near to God and cling to His promises. Turn from a life lived for selfish gain. Allow the Holy Spirit to cleanse you from the inside out. You have a destiny and a purpose only you can fulfill. Walk in obedience to your calling.

Heavenly Father,

Thank You for pursuing me even when I am walking in disobedience. Cleanse me of all my iniquities and give me a heart that is bent toward obedience in all that I say and do. You are my strength and my salvation. You are faithful to keep Your promises. I want to live my life walking in obedience to my calling.

In Jesus's mighty name, Amen

LIVING BY THE SPIRIT: OBEDIENCE, TRANSFORMATION, AND FRUITFULNESS

I want to encourage you to seek God first and let the Holy Spirit guide you in all truth. Living by faith and walking in God's goodness and obedience will result in a fruitful life.

Did you know that when you live in obedience, others will begin to see external changes in your life, which will overflow from your internal transformation? They will recognize you by your fruit. Matthew 7:16–20 says: "By their fruit you will recognize them. Do people pick grapes from thornbushes, or figs from thistles? Likewise, every good tree bears good fruit, but a bad tree bears bad fruit. A good tree cannot bear bad fruit, and a bad tree cannot bear good fruit. Every tree that does not bear good fruit is cut down and thrown into the fire. Thus, by their fruit you will recognize them."

The Bible uses fruit as a metaphor representing the outward manifestation of a person's faith. In this passage, Jesus teaches us that we can identify false prophets by their actions. Just as a tree is known by its fruit, a person's life and works reveal whether their teachings are truly from God. The more you read and study the Bible and the teachings of Jesus, the more you will recognize false teachers and gain a deeper understanding of the truth.

Are you living like you believe what you believe? Are your actions and words aligning with your beliefs? Your faith put into action reflects your beliefs.

Are you bearing good fruit?

The Holy Spirit guides us into all truth. John 16:13 says: "But when he, the Spirit of truth, comes, he will guide you into all the truth. He will not speak on his own; he will speak only what he hears, and he will tell you what is yet to come." This verse promises the Holy Spirit's presence and work in us, helping us understand God's truth fully in our personal lives and in our understanding of the world.

How do we know if we are reflecting all truth in our lives? What is the fruit we should bear to others? This fruit is a reflection of your belief. Galatians 5:22–23 tells us: "But the fruit of the Spirit is love, joy, peace, forbearance, kindness, goodness, faithfulness, gentleness and self-control. Against such things there is no law." This is a list of virtues you will produce and display when you are living according to the Holy Spirit. You will display these gifts of the Holy Spirit when you live in obedience and walk in all truth. This fruit is reflected in your life as a believer as you walk in God's commands.

My life did not reflect the fruit of the Spirit until I believed and loved the Lord with all my heart, mind, soul, and strength. I loved things according to my flesh. I believed in a false god—a god that fit into my needs and desires. I loved myself more than God and those in my inner circle. I had faith in something I truly didn't understand or comprehend. It was a long journey of faith, but I know that each step taught me more about who I am and who I belong to—Jesus. His love for you and me runs so deep that nothing I say will ever explain it. It's incomprehensible. The grace of God is matchless. His love and favor are an endless gift given to His children. You and I are heirs to a kingdom we do not deserve, but because of His kindness, mercy, and grace, we are eternally royalty in His house.

I was listening to a sermon recently, and the pastor said, "If you fix your thoughts on God, God fixes your thoughts." The Lord pursues us and leads us back to Him. Spend time praying and studying the Word of God.

It is so important to have a positive mindset fixed on God's truths and a deep relationship with the Lord. The Holy Spirit will guide you and lead you in all truth.

MAKING IT ABOUT ME

Message: *Walking in obedience to God leads to a fruitful life.* Read the following Scriptures and meditate on these truths for a while. Let them simmer in your spirit before moving on.

> Matthew 7:16–20: "By their fruit you will recognize them. Do people pick grapes from thornbushes, or figs from thistles? Likewise, every good tree bears good fruit, but a bad tree bears bad fruit. A good tree cannot bear bad fruit, and a bad tree cannot bear good fruit. Every tree that does not bear good fruit is cut down and thrown into the fire. Thus, by their fruit you will recognize them."

> John 16:13: "But when he, the Spirit of truth, comes, he will guide you into all the truth. He will not speak on his own; he will speak only what he hears, and he will tell you what is yet to come."

> Galatians 5:22–23: "But the fruit of the Spirit is love, joy, peace, forbearance, kindness, goodness, faithfulness, gentleness and self-control. Against such things there is no law."

Missional: Take a few moments and reflect on areas of your life that are not aligning with God's promises. What are some things that hold you back from the fruit God wants to grow in your life? What fruit do you struggle to bear? What are you doing to keep in step with the Holy Spirit?

Meditate: I pray you spend time with the Lord, allowing your eyes to be fixed on Him. Trust in His plans for you. He will transform you and lead you to your kingdom purpose.

Heavenly Father,

Thank You for guiding me into all truth. Help me see the things that are not bearing good fruit in my life. Transform me and lead me in Your ways. I want to bear good fruit in my life. I want to be recognized by my good fruit so I may bring You glory in all I do.

In Jesus's name, Amen

FROM SUFFERING TO SPIRITUAL GROWTH: EMBRACING GOD'S WILL

I want to encourage you to trust in God's plan and submit to His will for your life. Have faith, knowing that the goodness of God will work everything out for your good.

Do you ever sit in silence and ponder the meaning of it all? Do you wrestle with God to try to understand the meaning of grief and sorrow? Do you wonder why we must go through suffering after suffering and hardship after hardship in life? Why can't we just live in peace and harmony and enjoy the fruits of our labor? Why can't our faith carry us into only serene and harmonious living without ever having to go through trials? Is there purpose in our pain? I have pondered this in my own life and wrestled with the same questions: Why must we suffer and endure hardships, and is there purpose in it all?

The apostle Paul had a life full of trials and tribulations as he proclaimed the gospel to the gentiles, yet he endured hardships with joy and contentment. He endured such things as beatings, near-death experiences, and imprisonment. Paul writes in Philippians 4:11–13, "I am not saying this because I am in need, for I have learned to be content whatever the circumstances. I know what it is to be in need, and I know what it is to have plenty. I have learned the secret of being content in any and every situation, whether well fed or hungry, whether living in plenty or in want. I can do all this through him who gives me strength." True contentment is possible for us in Christ. Contentment doesn't come from outside of us, nor from our circumstances, but inside of us through our relationship with Christ.

Hardships can be endured with joy when we have our eyes fixed on the hope set before us in Christ Jesus. Our faith gives us the strength to endure as we lean on the power of the Holy Spirit to guide us through the pain. We can have joy knowing that even though we suffer, there is an eternal hope in Jesus. In Romans 8:18, the apostle Paul writes, "I consider that our present sufferings are not worth comparing with the glory that will be revealed in us." This passage brings us hope in knowing the eternal glory awaiting us in our future.

We can rest assured in our suffering that there is an eternal hope awaiting us. But there is more. When we endure trials of many kinds, there is an eternal purpose in our pain. We are being refined from the inside out. Second Corinthians 4:16 tells us, "Therefore we do not lose heart. Though outwardly we are wasting away, yet inwardly we are being renewed day by day." We are being renewed through faith and the work of the Holy Spirit, allowing us to endure hardships while keeping our gaze on eternal glory.

We can do all things through Christ who strengthens us. The Lord works in and through us as we endure the difficulties of life. He never promised us a life free of pain. How would we know the depths and heights of true contentment and joy if we never had to feel pain and suffering in life?

It is hard to comprehend joy in the midst of suffering. Who wants to suffer and go through trials for longer than a minute? It is hard to understand when we are in the pain. We just want to pray it away. We want to get back to our normal routines. We want respite from the pain. We don't want to endure any longer than we have to. We are not going to fully understand the why in every trial, especially when we are in the middle of the pain and discomfort. But we can be confident in knowing that the Lord is with us amid the pain. His presence allows us to endure it, knowing it will produce redeeming grace in abundance. James 1:2–4 says, "Consider it pure joy, my brothers and sisters, whenever you face trials of many kinds, because you know that the testing of your faith produces perseverance. Let perseverance finish its work so that you may be mature and complete, not lacking anything." Trials will produce perseverance as you endure the testing of your faith, and this will bring spiritual completeness. We must view trials as opportunities for spiritual growth leading us to mature faith. Facing trials with a positive attitude can lead to joy amid the hardship.

I have faced trials of many kinds in my own life. I have walked through grief, health issues, relational hardships, infertility, and financial difficulties. I can attest that I wanted every trial to end quickly. I wrestled with God amid the suffering and asked the question, "Why?" I did not understand the depths and reasons for my suffering until I had a deep relationship with the Lord. I gained clarity on the other side of each trial. I have grown spiritually and see the purpose in my pain. This took a great deal of faith, perseverance, and a positive attitude. I now view my trials differently and see my pain and suffering through the lens of faith. I walk through my circumstances with a positive attitude and view them as an opportunity to bring glory to God amid the peaks and valleys of life.

MAKING IT ABOUT ME

Message: *Submit to God's plan and trust He is working everything out for your good.* Read the following Scriptures and meditate on these truths for a while. Let them simmer in your spirit before moving on.

> Romans 8:18: "I consider that our present sufferings are not worth comparing with the glory that will be revealed in us."

> 2 Corinthians 4:16: "Therefore we do not lose heart. Though outwardly we are wasting away, yet inwardly we are being renewed day by day."

> James 1:2–4: "Consider it pure joy, my brothers and sisters, whenever

you face trials of many kinds, because you know that the testing of
your faith produces perseverance. Let perseverance finish its work
so that you may be mature and complete, not lacking anything."

Missional: Take a few moments to reflect on the trials you are facing and
write down how you can find joy in each one. How has God revealed Himself in these areas of your life? Where do you need to let go, have faith, and
give it to God?

Meditate: I pray you reflect on the trials of your life through the lens of faith.
Trust in the will of God and count it pure joy when you face hardships. You
are being renewed for a greater purpose.

Heavenly Father,

*Thank You for allowing me to face trials with perseverance. You
are my strength and my strong tower in every struggle. Help me to
continue to see trials through the lens of faith. I trust in Your will and
goodness in my life. Your ways are higher and greater than mine.*

In Jesus's name, Amen

FINDING JOY IN WHAT YOU HAVE: A LESSON IN FAITH AND PROVISION

I want to encourage you today to hold on to the confession of your faith. Live life knowing the Lord will never leave you nor forsake you. His plan is always better.

Do you hold on to your life so tightly that the thought of a new direction or path leaves you feeling anxious or riddled with worry? Do you find yourself living for a future hope that is secure in stuff? A sense of "when I get this" or "get there," "I will be happy and content"? Does money drive your happiness, or the lack of money determine your worth? We live in a culture that tells us more is better, and we are not living life to the fullest if we do not have the latest and greatest stuff. We are all guilty of wanting what we do not have. The secret is being content with what we do have. Yes, we need money to live, but we do not need to live for money. Are you able to love God and money in synchrony?

In my adolescent years, I wanted everything and did not understand why I couldn't have what my friends had. It was a struggle for my teenage self. I wanted to be rich, to have all the things money could buy. My parents lived a meek life. We did not live in a fancy house or drive an expensive car. My parents barely made ends meet. So this was my conundrum: How could I have the things I wanted without money? I remember praying at eleven and testing my faith before the throne of grace. I asked God for money to give me my heart's desires, and if He didn't, He was not real. Well, I learned a valuable lesson that day. I did not get money, but I did get my heart's deepest desire—faith in a real God. The Scripture the Lord showed me was Matthew 6:24: "No one can serve two masters. Either you will hate the one and love the other, or you will be devoted to the one and despise the other. You cannot serve both God and money."

The root of all evil is the *love* of money. It's not that we can't have money; it just can't be our master. Everything we have is not ours, anyway. It is a gift from God. All blessings come from above. We came into this life with nothing and will leave with nothing, but all the gifts in between are given to us by God. How we steward them matters. Do you give your resources to better the kingdom of God? Do you serve others extravagantly to bring glory to God? Do you live your life with a kingdom mindset, pursuing things that are pleasing to God rather than yourself? Do you live by faith, walking in God's promises while abandoning the conformity of this world? Do you trust God's provision for you?

Let's look at Matthew 6:26–27: "Look at the birds of the air; they do not sow or reap or store away in barns, and yet your heavenly Father feeds them. Are you not much more valuable than they? Can any one of you by worrying add a single hour to your life?" This Scripture is one that brings me the most comfort when I am struggling to trust God and His provision for me. If He feeds the birds daily and they do not fret or store up their treasure, how much more will He feed His child? There is no need to worry about tomorrow since we have a faithful provider and sustainer of all things.

The Scripture goes on in verses 28–30: "And why do you worry about clothes? See how the flowers of the field grow. They do not labor or spin. Yet I tell you that not even Solomon in all his splendor was dressed like one of these. If that is how God clothes the grass of the field, which is here today and tomorrow is thrown into the fire, will he not much more clothe you— you of little faith?" We must trust in God's plans for us. He knows what we need, and He will provide for us in His timing.

MAKING IT ABOUT ME

Message: *Live for the things that bring faithful provision in your life.* Read the following Scriptures and meditate on these truths for a while. Let them simmer in your spirit before moving on.

> Matthew 6:26–27: "Look at the birds of the air; they do not sow or reap or store away in barns, and yet your heavenly Father feeds them. Are you not much more valuable than they? Can any one of you by worrying add a single hour to your life?"

> Matthew 6:28–30: "And why do you worry about clothes? See how the flowers of the field grow. They do not labor or spin. Yet I tell you that not even Solomon in all his splendor was dressed like one of these. If that is how God clothes the grass of the field, which is here today and tomorrow is thrown into the fire, will he not much more clothe you—you of little faith?"

Missional: Take a few moments and reflect on how God has provided for you. Write down five things God has provided in your life that you asked for that have been a blessing. How has that brought you comfort or stability in your life? What are some ways you can walk in obedience to God's will today?

Meditate: I pray you cling to your faith and let go of the things of this world. There is a purpose and a plan that far exceeds anything you could ever ask or imagine. Walking in obedience leads you to true contentment and lasting joy.

Heavenly Father,

Thank You for teaching me and leading me to the things that are good for me in my life. Help me to seek the things that lead me to my purpose and Your provisions for me. Your steadfast love endures forever.

In Jesus's name, Amen

RESTING IN GOD'S GOODNESS AND GRACE

I want to encourage you to draw near to the Lord and let your heart rest in His goodness and trust He has a plan for your life.

Are you living a life worthy of the gospel? Do you let the love of God's grace lead your heart? Are you someone who feels like you're not good enough to be loved, or you lack the ability to just rest in the goodness of God without having to strive to please the Lord? Did you know the grace of God is enough? Are you living like you believe what you believe? A life empowered by obedience?

In the Bible, grace is predominantly defined as God's unmerited favor and love extended to humanity. It is a gift given by God, and His favor is bestowed upon us in various ways: through salvation, forgiveness, and the empowerment to live a godly life.

It's hard to believe we are given something so beautiful and that nothing we do can change how much grace we are given. Jesus died for those He loves—even those who did not and do not love Him in return. Jesus shows love and compassion to sinners who deserve His punishment. His kindness is extended to everyone. His grace is sufficient and is enough in every circumstance. Mercy is displayed and grace is given to us through Jesus Christ.

John 1:16–17 tells us: "Out of his fullness we have all received grace in place of grace already given. For the law was given through Moses; grace and truth came through Jesus Christ." Grace is lavished on the believer through Jesus

Christ. You are given the greatest gift when you have salvation through Jesus Christ: the gift of grace. That means you did not earn this gift; you received it by grace alone. It was freely given to you. Your behavior does not determine your rewards from above. Rest in that truth. Nothing you do or will do can change what has been given to you by the blood of Jesus. Your works and your behavior do not change your destiny in the kingdom of heaven. You were sealed at your salvation. You are a chosen child of God. Knowing the goodness and faithfulness of God will transform how you live your life—a life that is bent on serving and honoring the Lord from within, and His grace will overflow and extend to those around you. A thankful heart will drive you to obedience.

Titus 2:11–12 (ESV) says, "For the grace of God has appeared, bringing salvation for all people, training us to renounce ungodliness and worldly passions, and to live self-controlled, upright, and godly lives in the present age." This passage emphasizes that grace not only saves but also instructs and empowers believers to live a righteous life. Grace empowers us to obedience. Grace leads us to live a holy and righteous life. Your heart is being renewed and sanctified day by day by the Holy Spirit.

I struggled for a long time to understand that I did not need to strive to please God. My behavior did not determine God's love for me. Early in my walk, I would do things to try to earn favor with God. I never felt I could live up to His goodness. I battled within my mind for a long time. Outwardly, I appeared to be what some would call a "good Christian." I was going to church regularly, attending Bible studies, and serving in my church as well. Inwardly, I was struggling with sinful patterns, and my mind could not rest. It was constantly bombarded with intrusive thoughts, and I lived for selfish gain. This was a cycle, but God, who is rich in mercy, never gave up on me. He pursued me and led me through a series of events to surrender my will and repent. His kindness led me to repentance. His grace was always there; I just was not aware of it. I started going deeper in my relationship with Him through the disciplines of the faith. The more I spent time with the Lord, the more my heart was renewed and transformed. I am thankful for His grace that is always being lavished upon me. His grace is sufficient for me. His power is made perfect in my weakness. I am bent toward pursuing a life lived for Jesus—a life lived for kingdom purposes. I can testify to the goodness of God, and His steadfast love endures forever.

MAKING IT ABOUT ME

Message: *Rest in God's goodness and grace.* Read the following Scriptures and meditate on these truths for a while. Let them simmer in your spirit before moving on.

> John 1:16–17: "Out of his fullness we have all received grace in place of grace already given. For the law was given through Moses; grace and truth came through Jesus Christ."

> Titus 2:11–12 (ESV): "For the grace of God has appeared, bringing salvation for all people, training us to renounce ungodliness and worldly passions, and to live self-controlled, upright, and godly lives in the present age."

Missional: Take a few moments and reflect on the love and grace the Lord has blessed you with over your life. Where do you see evidence of God's grace in your life? Write down areas of your life where you need to let go and trust the Lord and His provisions for you.

Meditate: I pray you seek the Lord with all your heart and rest in His goodness and grace today.

Heavenly Father,

Thank You for Your grace and mercy that You lavish upon me daily. Help me let go of the things that make me worry and strive for more. I want to turn from my sin and live a life in obedience to Your will. You are my rock and my salvation.

In Jesus's name, Amen

ABILITY

ABILITY—LIVING AN OBEDIENT LIFE
ENGAGING IN THE DISCIPLINES OF THE FAITH.

*So then, just as you received Christ Jesus as Lord, continue to live
your lives in him, rooted and built up in him, strengthened in the
faith as you were taught, and overflowing with thankfulness.*

COLOSSIANS 2:6–7

Ability is turning from a life of selfish gain and walking out your faith with a thankful servant's heart. Alistair Begg says, "God is pleased when all our days and duties are marked by gratitude … the believer will stand out as a light in a dark place by displaying a thankful heart." We are called to live a life of gratitude and thanksgiving, praising the Lord through the circumstances of life and believing that God is always working everything for His good purposes. When we create space in our lives to help others, we will see change as grace and blessings flow through us. Your walk will strengthen the faith of those around you. Your testimony becomes medicine to those hurting and struggling. We must act in faith and let go of the things that hinder us from walking in obedience to the call on our lives.

A WELL OF HOPE, PEACE, AND JOY

I want to encourage you today to draw from the well that never runs dry—Jesus. His living water is for you and me. This water quenches the thirsty soul.

Have you ever been so thirsty for something, but once you get it, you just are not satisfied? It does not give lasting relief, and you try something else and find yourself searching yet again. Searching for something to bring you comfort, and yes, that peace we all long for. Some of us try to find it in food; others try to find it in substances like alcohol, and some try to find it in relationships with others. Many of us these days try to find it on social media. We are all searching for something or someone that takes us deeper, keeps us satisfied, and does not lose its luster over time. We must ask ourselves this: Do we long for something greater than ourselves? Do we want to understand the depths or the root of why we do what we do?

So the question becomes, where do you find your comfort? What are you always thirsting for?

The first thing that comes to my mind is sweets. I *love* chocolate. I can eat a whole meal and still want something sweet. This craving and desire never seem to be satisfied. I can go days without it, but then it hits me. I start to get the nagging desire for some chocolatey goodness. I grab a treat and quench my craving. But it is only satisfied temporarily. This is a constant battle, trying to find lasting satisfaction and comfort in something that keeps me wanting more. More of something that never seems to satisfy. I can also use social media to drown myself in mindless comfort and easily spend an hour or two scrolling down the pit of comparison, always trying to get satisfaction from the reels of others, which we all know are not the real deal. Social media appears to be filled with a better version of us, which can leave us unsatisfied, longing for something more—something we can't attain.

One of my favorite stories in the Bible comes from John 4—the woman at the well. I have heard so many sermons and so much commentary on this story. I always get emotional, especially when I read this Scripture. It speaks to my very soul. Just like the woman at the well, we all have parts of us we want to hide from the world—those parts no one knows, the depths and degree of our past that we try to forget, the inner voice that tells us we are not worthy and condemns us. The woman at the well was trying to draw water at noon so no one would see her. No one could confront her. She was hiding her guilt and shame. She was comfortable there. Jesus shows up and changes everything for her. He tells her all the secrets she was hiding. He knew and still loved her. She was set free! He gave her His "living water," the water that never runs dry. John 4:14 says, "Whoever drinks the water I give them will never thirst. Indeed, the water I give them will become in them a spring of water welling up to eternal life." Jesus shifts the conversation from physical thirst to a deeper, spiritual thirst, offering "living water" as the answer. Jesus offers us a well of hope, a well of peace, a well of joy, and a well of eternity. Jesus offers us salvation. He offers us the gift of grace.

Isaiah 12:2–3 says, " 'Surely God is my salvation; I will trust and not be afraid. The LORD, the LORD himself, is my strength and my defense; he has become my salvation.' With joy you will draw water from the wells of salvation." God provides the means for our rescue, the power to endure, and the experience of joy. We must put our faith in God, even when we are afraid. The visual of drawing water from wells to convey the joy of salvation expresses that God's presence and provisions are obtainable by everyone who searches for them. Seek the Lord in all you do and trust in His promises. He is your well of hope, peace, and joy.

MAKING IT ABOUT ME

Message: *Seek the water that never runs dry.* Read the following Scriptures and meditate on these truths for a while. Let them simmer in your spirit before moving on.

> John 4:14: "Whoever drinks the water I give them will never thirst. Indeed, the water I give them will become in them a spring of water welling up to eternal life."

> Isaiah 12:2–3: " 'Surely God is my salvation; I will trust and not be afraid. The LORD, the LORD himself, is my strength and my defense; he has become my salvation.' With joy you will draw water from the wells of salvation."

Missional: Take a few moments and reflect on the areas of your life that are "dry." What brings you temporal comfort or relief but does not satisfy your soul? Write down three things that bring you joy and draw you close to God. Take a few moments and spend time with the Lord and ask Him to help you cleanse your soul with His living water.

Meditate: I pray you never get thirsty for the things of this world. I pray you find comfort and lasting satisfaction in the one who holds the water that will bring you everlasting life—Jesus.

Heavenly Father,

Thank You for Your living water. You are the well that never leaves me dry. Help me seek You first in all that I do, rather than the things of this world that leave me unsatisfied, searching for comfort and peace. You are my joy and my salvation. I want to trust You more and let go of this world. Give me the ability and strength to continue to seek Your goodness all my days.

In Jesus's name, Amen

FACING YOUR GOLIATH

I want to encourage you today to face your Goliath with the victory that has already been won for you. Do you ever feel like you're constantly in a battle? A battle you just don't feel equipped to win? Do you ever get the sense that something or someone is out to get you, and that you just can't catch a break? You know that feeling—when it rains, it pours. You know when you're facing a battle that is beyond your ability to handle with your own strength, or when you don't have the tools for the battle. I think a better question to ask is, how do you get beyond the battle to face your giant and win? That's something I am learning as I face the battles in this world. I attack my giant differently now than I did before I understood my position in Christ. I used to go into a battle defeated before I even started to fight. I would try to fight in my own strength and expect a victorious outcome without even understanding the battle and the purpose behind it.

The purpose or lesson from God doesn't always surface amid the battle. The purpose, lesson, and blessings typically come after the battle, when your giant is defeated. You will see God's provision and providence more clearly. That is where the most change occurs in our lives—when we realize the battle was a means to a greater end. You are victorious in Him.

Our battles are given to us to refine and grow our faith, or sometimes we face battles that are just a consequence of living in a fallen world. We read this in Genesis 3, when the snake enters the garden of Eden. What matters isn't why the battle occurs but that we have the tools needed for battle when we put our trust and faith in God. He fights our battles. "The one who is in you is greater than the one who is in the world" (1 John 4:4).

Years ago, I read a book called *Victory in Spiritual Warfare: Outfitting Yourself for the Battle.* The author, Tony Evans, states, "If all you see is what you see, you do not see all there is to be seen." We do not battle with flesh and blood, but with principalities and darkness in the unseen, spiritual realm.

"For our struggle is not against flesh and blood, but against the rulers, against the authorities, against the powers of this dark world" (Eph. 6:12).

Our giants feel physical, but there is always a spiritual part to our battle. We may not know or understand it, but it is there, and we must continue to draw near to the One who already won the battle for us—Jesus. Colossians 2:15 (ESV) says, "He disarmed the rulers and authorities and put them to open shame, by triumphing over them in him."

Let's look at the life of David before he was king. David was a boy with a small physical stature and was not fit to fight any physical battle and win, let alone a giant. How was he prepared to face a giant that had greater power and stamina? How did he kill the giant with just a sling and a stone? It seems so unlikely, but that is exactly the position God put him in and prepared him for long before he faced that battle. I encourage you to read the entire story in the book of 1 Samuel. I am going to share how God prepared him and gave him the victory over the biggest physical giant he would face, Goliath. He prepared David through his life experiences as a shepherd. It was God's providence in David's life. David worked for his father by tending sheep as a young boy. He had to kill bears and lions with a sling and a stone in the field. It is what he knew and how he defeated his giants—the animals. When David was about to battle Goliath, he was put in full physical armor, but he did not feel comfortable because it was too big and not the right fit for him to fight this battle. He wanted to use the tools the Lord prepared him with all his life. He wanted to use just a sling and a stone, with no physical armor but with the armor of God. The armor that fights every battle and wins. First Samuel 17:37 says, "The LORD who rescued me from the paw of the lion and the paw of the bear will rescue me from the hand of this Philistine." You see, the very tool he used prior to the battle was his preparation with a bear and a lion. God prepared him before he faced his giant. I bet there were many small battles David faced that ultimately prepared him to battle Goliath. God also does this with us in our lives.

We each have a Goliath. We face giants every day. Our giants may be financial, relational, or physical. The ones that seems to be the toughest and most difficult to overcome are our emotional giants. Our emotions tend to get out of control in the midst of any battle we face. The battle of our minds is a Goliath that is the toughest to defeat. These are the giants that are hidden, the ones we try to fight alone. I know those giants just get bigger and harder to fight in your own strength. The good news is that we have a God who gives us the strength and courage to face our battles with Him by our side. He will never leave you nor forsake you, even when it seems too much to bear. He will give you what you need in His perfect timing. God is always on time. Joshua 1:9 (ESV) tells us, "Have I not commanded you? Be strong and courageous. Do not be frightened, and do not be dismayed, for the LORD your God is with you wherever you go." The Lord has given you His armor, His weapons, and His tools specific to your journey and the battles you have faced and will face.

There is a song by Elevation Worship called "Always on Time" that encourages me. The lyrics remind me of how God always works it out, even in the darkest and toughest trials. He is always on time. His timing is perfect.

MAKING IT ABOUT ME

Message: *God is with you in every battle.* Read the following Scriptures and meditate on these truths for a while. Let them simmer in your spirit before moving on.

> Ephesians 6:12: "For our struggle is not against flesh and blood, but against the rulers, against the authorities, against the powers of this dark world."

1 John 4:4: "The one who is in you is greater than the one who is in the world."

1 Samuel 17:37: "The LORD who rescued me from the paw of the lion and the paw of the bear will rescue me from the hand of this Philistine."

Joshua 1:9 (ESV): "Have I not commanded you? Be strong and courageous. Do not be frightened, and do not be dismayed, for the LORD your God is with you wherever you go."

Missional: Take a few moments and reflect on the power of God and His sovereignty over His children. Write down the battles you are facing right now. Give those to God and be still, knowing He fights your battles and is with you wherever you go.

Meditate: I pray you find comfort and strength in your darkest trials. God sees *you*. God *knows* your struggle. God is with *you*. You can face your Goliaths with *Him*.

Heavenly Father,

Thank You for fighting my battles even when I do not see them. You are always working things out for my good and Your glory. I give You all my struggles and trials, and I release my control over them. I am trusting in Your sovereignty and goodness over my life. You are my giant in my battles, and You are my strength and victory.

In Jesus's mighty name, Amen

HE IS BIGGER
THAN YOUR STORM

I want to encourage you and empower you to be a blessing to someone today. I was going through an old drawer by my prayer wall the other day and stumbled upon a book that brought back some beautiful memories of how God used it to help me in my classroom as a teacher during a difficult season.

The book is called *Cow in the Dark* by Todd Aaron Smith. It's a story about a time when there was a big storm at a farm. A rumor started that there was a monster outside. As the rumor was passed on to the other animals in the barn, the story grew bigger and bigger! Everyone was so afraid. During the adventure, everyone learned an important lesson through the actions of a little sheep: that there is nothing to be afraid of, even in the dark! You see, the sheep knew what the farm animals didn't. The sheep knew God is bigger than anything that might be out in the dark. He is in the dark *with* us.

Whatever storm or dark place you may find yourself in, just know that the Lord is with you, and He will give you the strength and the courage to face your storm.

I am reminded of Isaiah 41:10: "Do not fear, for I am with you; do not be dismayed, for I am your God. I will strengthen you and help you; I will uphold you with my righteous right hand." The Lord washed this Scripture over me not too long ago when I had an unforeseen accident and was in the hospital with a minor brain injury. I remember feeling such peace amid the chaos.

What I learned from this was that storms will come and go in our lives, and when they do (and they will), hold on to God's promises through them. Rest in the assurance that Jesus is with you and will keep you safe.

Jesus is the only one who can give us the strength to keep calm and weather the storm. He is with us *through* the storm.

I pray that you and I can have peace, strength, and courage like that little sheep, sleeping while all the other farm animals were in a panic over the monster in the dark. Eventually, the farm animals realized that the monster was nothing but the noise from the wind.

It's funny how we can do the same thing with the challenges and trials we face. Sometimes the loud noise in our lives can become louder and bigger than it really is. We can create a storm that overwhelms us and leaves us feeling afraid and anxious.

I am here to encourage you today to fix your eyes on Jesus and off your storm. He will walk with you through it. Rest in His presence today and know you are His sheep, and you are safe. He is your good shepherd.

MAKING IT ABOUT ME

Message: *God is bigger than your storm.* Read the following Scripture and meditate on this truth for a while. Let it simmer in your spirit before moving on.

> Isaiah 41:10: "Do not fear, for I am with you; do not be dismayed, for I am your God. I will strengthen you and help you; I will uphold you with my righteous right hand."

Missional: Take a few moments and reflect on how God has brought you through difficult seasons in your life. Now write down the things you are worried about in this season of life and release them to the Lord in prayer.

Meditate: I pray He will lead you to still waters and greener pastures. Just rest in Him.

Heavenly Father,

Thank You for being my good shepherd, leading me down the path of peace and stillness with You. I ask that You calm the storms in my life as I navigate through them with You by my side. You tell me in Your Word that I was not given a spirit of fear, but of power, love, and a sound mind. Keep my eyes fixed on You in the middle of every storm and guide me to still water.

In Jesus's name, Amen

A GIFT OF GRATITUDE

I want to encourage you today to keep your heart filled with gratitude. It will change your attitude and lead you to a life filled with joy in every circumstance.

Did you know that scientific research shows you can't experience anxiety while practicing gratitude? It makes perfect sense to me. If you look at this from a biblical worldview, I'm reminded of a couple of Scriptures.

Philippians 4:6 says, "Do not be anxious about anything, but in every situation, by prayer and petition, with thanksgiving, present your requests to God."

This passage encourages Christians to replace worry with prayerful trust in God, suggesting that God's peace serves as a protective force for mental and emotional well-being. It also emphasizes the importance of bringing all personal concerns—whether physical, spiritual, or relational—to God through prayer.

If you read further, Philippians 4:8 states, "Finally, brothers and sisters, whatever is true, whatever is noble, whatever is right, whatever is pure, whatever is lovely, whatever is admirable—if anything is excellent or praiseworthy—think about such things."

The passage urges believers to cultivate a mindset centered on positive and uplifting qualities.

In everyday life, this principle is applied by consciously directing one's thoughts to virtuous ideas and the positive attributes of people and events, thus promoting a more constructive mental space.

Gratitude can help you focus on the present and break negative thought patterns. You make a conscious choice every morning when you wake up. What are you going to focus your mind on today? Are you going to wake up with an attitude or wake up with gratitude?

You can choose to wake up grumpy and focus your attention on the mountain set before you each day. You know, the mountain of to-do lists, the work you must do, or the people you have to deal with every day who are not easy to get along with. I know you can easily start your day in a negative state of mind. It's not hard to do. There is so much negativity in the world that you can easily become anxious. But *you* can change your focus each day. You can choose to wake up with a grateful heart. You can thank God for every blessing you have before your toes even touch the floor.

Yes, waking up with gratitude sets your mind on the things that center you on the goodness all around you. It is there in the things we take for granted, like the breath in our lungs, the sun rising each day, and the relationships we get to cultivate.

What are you grateful for today? How can you keep your mindset uplifting and positive toward yourself and others?

Prayer is the first thing that comes to my mind—trusting in the Lord to work out the details in my life, letting go, and giving it to God to work out. That is not easy—giving up your will and control to obey His will, surrendering all to Jesus. I have been in many hard places in my life where I wanted to just give up on others or crawl into a corner and hide, sheltering myself away from the world—my safe place. I sat in spaces that were unbearable and wondered, *Why is this so hard? Where is God in this?* I know you have been there too. Life can be difficult, and it can be hard to simply breathe. I can tell you that when I prayed, let it go, and surrendered my control, I began to see God work in my situation or circumstance. It was not always an easy fix, and some of my prayers are still unanswered. I know that His will and timing are perfect. I have learned to praise in the waiting. The waiting is where God teaches and refines.

I read a book years ago called *One Thousand Gifts* by Ann Voskamp. This quote resonated with me when I read it: "The brave who focus on all things good and all things beautiful and all things true, even in the small, who give thanks for it and discover joy even in the here and now, they are the change agents who bring fullest Light to all the world."

Be brave and continue to focus your mind on all that is good. You will see change, and more importantly, you will be a light of change in the world around you.

I purposely left out the Scripture verse in between the two I shared. I wanted to leave you with the most important part of praying and having a grateful heart. Philippians 4:7 says, "And the peace of God, which transcends all understanding, will guard your hearts and your minds in Christ Jesus."

When you get peace, it transcends your human understanding. It's a gift from God that guards your heart from anxiety and fear.

MAKING IT ABOUT ME

Message: *A grateful heart is a joyful heart.* Read the following Scriptures and meditate on these truths for a while. Let them simmer in your spirit before moving on.

> Philippians 4:6: "Do not be anxious about anything, but in every situation, by prayer and petition, with thanksgiving, present your requests to God."

> Philippians 4:8: "Finally, brothers and sisters, whatever is true, whatever is noble, whatever is right, whatever is pure, whatever is lovely, whatever is admirable—if anything is excellent or praiseworthy—think about such things."

> Philippians 4:7: "And the peace of God, which transcends all understanding, will guard your hearts and your minds in Christ Jesus."

Missional: Take a few moments and reflect on the gifts in your life. Write down as many gifts as you can think of that God has blessed you with. Thank God for the many blessings that you see or you don't see Him working out in your life. He is a faithful God.

Meditate: I pray you have this kind of peace. It is a deep and supernatural kind of peace that carries you through the most difficult circumstances and keeps your mind on Him and not the pain or suffering this world can bring. It leads you to a grateful heart. Your joy is complete in Him.

Heavenly Father,

Thank You for Your guidance and grace in my life. I am grateful for all my blessings. I am thankful for the prayers answered and unanswered because I know You are working out everything for my good and Your glory. You are the God of peace.

In Jesus's name, Amen

LIVING BY FAITH: A GIFT AND A JOURNEY

I want to encourage you today to choose faith over fear.

The object of our faith determines what actions we will take in any circumstance. Do you have faith as small as a mustard seed? Is your faith determined by your ability to conquer a situation? What do you put your faith in? Does your fear have the victory in your life? Do you have faith over fear?

I am reminded of the first time I had real faith, the kind of faith that changes you. I was eleven years old, praying in the back seat of my parents' car. We were on our way to a store that was going out of business, and I wanted to buy something, but my parents were adamant and would not budge on giving me the money I wanted. So I decided I would pray, because I was taught that is what you do when you want something and can't get it in your own strength. My prayer went something like this: *Dear God, I want to find money on the ground, and if I do not find it, well, You are not real and You do not exist. Amen.*

I remember getting out of the car, looking on the ground, and when I got into the store, looking all around on the floor to see if God blessed my prayer. I looked down and saw a small, dirty piece of paper the size of a dollar. I felt a strong nudge inside to pick it up. I turned the paper over, and to this day I only remember part of what was on it. I remember the words "You do not know the one who sent me," and "Do not put your God to a test. You cannot have two masters, love and money." The words were in red. I threw the paper down after reading it twice. I had a reverent kind of fear come over me. I didn't share that story for years. But it was the first time I had genuine faith in the God who sees me. I later learned the Scripture was from Matthew 6:24, "No one can serve two masters. Either you will hate the one and love the other, or you will be devoted to the one and despise the other. You cannot serve both God and money."

This story changed everything for me. It is my faith story. It began my prayer life and my faith object—Jesus. I later learned how to trust and walk deeper with the Lord.

Faith is not something we attain. It is given to us by God. Ephesians 2:8–9 says, "For it is by grace you have been saved, through faith—and this is not from yourselves, it is the gift of God—not by works, so that no one can boast." This passage reveals that our salvation is a gift, not a reward, which brings confidence and stability in our connection with God. Faith is a gift that is nurtured and grown as we trust and walk deeper in relationship with Jesus. The Lord helps you on your faith journey with Him. The Bible tells us in Matthew 17:20, "Truly I tell you, if you have faith as small as a mustard seed, you can say to this mountain, 'Move from here to there,' and it will move. Nothing will be impossible for you." This is a reminder that God can work in you with even a small amount of faith.

My favorite quote about faith is from Pastor Tony Evans: "Faith is acting like it is so even when it is not so, in order that it might be so, simply because God said so." Our faith is based on God's Word. Faith is an action. There are practical ways to deepen your faith. Cling to the promises of God daily. Take time in your day to dedicate to prayer and worship. Read your Bible daily. Pick a Scripture or two to meditate on. Spend quiet time with Jesus. Get in a biblical community. Surround yourself with other Christians to stir each other up toward love and good deeds. Your faith can move mountains when you trust and act on the promises of God; your faith will move mountains. Let your faith move you in the direction of godliness.

How do we persevere through fear? Your actions of faith direct you to something greater than what you are afraid of. Fear does not come from God. Second Timothy 1:7 (NKJV) tells us, "For God has not given us a spirit of fear, but of power and of love and of a sound mind." Faith is powerful and leads us to a sound mind. In the Gospel of Matthew, specifically chapter 8, verses 23 through 27, there's a story about Jesus and his followers encountering a violent storm while sailing. During the storm, Jesus is asleep, and his disciples, terrified by the raging waves, wake him up. Jesus then commands the wind and the sea to be still, and immediately the storm subsides, leaving the disciples amazed. The disciples' moments of doubt even after experiencing Jesus firsthand highlight that faith is a continuous journey, not a constant state. But their correction shows that Jesus expects our trust. He demonstrated his ability to overcome storms by rescuing them, and that same power is available to us when we face trials like health issues, job setbacks, marital strife, and the pain of loss.

Stepping out of the "boat" in faith, leaving fear behind you, and keeping your eyes on Jesus as you walk out the promises of God will lead you to a faith-filled life.

Fear is a feeling, and faith is an assurance of things hoped for. Remember, fear is a liar. Faith draws you closer to your provisions that God has set before you. Persevere through struggles and trust in the promises of the Lord. Seek the Lord in all things; He will answer in His timing. Praise Him in the waiting. Your faith will move mountains.

MAKING IT ABOUT ME

Message: *Choose faith over fear.* Read the following Scriptures and meditate on these truths for a while. Let them simmer in your spirit before moving on.

> Matthew 6:24: "No one can serve two masters. Either you will hate the one and love the other, or you will be devoted to the one and despise the other. You cannot serve both God and money."

Ephesians 2:8–9: "For it is by grace you have been saved, through faith—and this is not from yourselves, it is the gift of God—not by works, so that no one can boast."

Missional: Take a few moments and reflect on how your faith has moved mountains in your life. What are some fears you need to face? Let go of your fears and the feelings attached to them and have faith God will move the mountains in your life.

Meditate: I pray you face your fears head-on, knowing that your faith will conquer them.

Heavenly Father,

Thank You for being my faith object. Your Word is the lamp to my feet and the light to my path. Help me discern the lies of the enemy and the voice of truth. I choose faith over fear. You are my defender and strong tower.

In Jesus's name, Amen

DAY 6

A CALL TO STILLNESS: RESTING IN THE LORD

I want to encourage you to sit and rest in Jesus today. Life can feel busy, and we can easily get distracted by so much noise. Even the good things we do can become a distraction from time spent with the Lord. I have been guilty of this in many seasons of my life.

As I write this, we are about to enter the season of Lent. For me, Lent has been a precious time with the Lord for over a decade. Lent is a special time for me to draw near to God and let go of the things that keep me from Him. I set aside a part of my day to give to the Lord for forty days, a retreat from my daily routines. I take time each day to sacrifice and spend time with the Lord. Each year it is different for me. This year, I will sacrifice my sleep in the morning to dwell in Scripture and walk a mile while spending time in prayer and worship. I also will sacrifice something that my flesh enjoys—sugar. It is just a reminder of the sacrifice Jesus gave for me, His life for mine. It keeps me centered each day on Him and His love for me. I do not consider Lent a work or something I do to earn favor from God. It is not a religious act for me. I participate in this season of Lent because of the love and grace the Lord has lavished upon me. I always look forward to it because I know I will intentionally rest in Him and be changed in some way.

If you do not participate in Lent or have a discipline of faith, how do you draw near to God? What does that look like in your daily life? Do you find peace in your day-to-day busyness? Do you find that even in silence your mind is racing with a million thoughts? Do your emotions take over? Do you find that you constantly are living with no sense of purpose or peace? Do you feel exhausted and emotionally drained every day, even though you rested physically at night?

If you're like me, it is hard to find moments to just sit and enjoy time to myself or just be still in the moment without thinking of all my to-do lists.

I remember a time in my life when I was completely overwhelmed with so much that it was hard to find rest for my soul. I could not quiet the internal noise in my mind. I would lay my head down after a busy day as a teacher, mom, and wife, and I would continually go over how I could have done things differently or think about what I needed to accomplish tomorrow. It was a cycle that caused so much fear and anxiousness. I am reminded of a Scripture the Lord washed over me more than ten years ago in a Lent season during deep meditative prayer with Him. It is Matthew 11:28–30 (ESV):

> Come to me, all who labor and are heavy laden, and I will give you rest. Take my yoke upon you, and learn from me, for I am gentle and lowly in heart, and you will find rest for your souls. For my yoke is easy, and my burden is light.

This was a profound and pivotal moment in my walk with the Lord. It changed everything, but I didn't know it at that time until I walked deeper and surrendered everything to Jesus. That meant repenting of all my sins and walking with Jesus and living life for Him. This was the beginning of my journey to live for the kingdom of God, on mission and serving others. I was given the gift of rest, a rest that I can't explain. Jesus took my burdens away, the burdens I could not let go of in my own strength. He gave me peace that surpassed all understanding, a peace that sustains me even in chaos. I didn't realize that the rest I was looking for was a deep and lasting rest only the Holy Spirit could bring me, a rest for my soul. This can be yours too.

I ask the question again. Do you have time set aside for the Lord each day? Do you have time in your day just to sit and rest in Him? I know it gets to be a challenge, especially as women who wear many hats, to take time for ourselves to just be alone and not feel guilty about it. Can I encourage you to take a moment of your day to just be still with the Lord? Think of it as your guilty pleasure. We can indulge in many things that are good for us, but this *good* thing can be life-changing and will have lasting benefits.

The Lord delights in us and wants us to spend time with Him. I know you will find rest there in the quiet with Him. He will give you restoration and nourishment for your soul.

I pray this Lent season is a time of rest for you and a time for you to draw near to Jesus. He loves you and is waiting for you.

MAKING IT ABOUT ME

Message: *Be still and REST in the Lord.* Read the following Scripture and meditate on this truth for a while. Let it simmer in your spirit before moving on.

> Matthew 11:28–30 (ESV): "Come to me, all who labor and are heavy laden, and I will give you rest. Take my yoke upon you, and learn from me, for I am gentle and lowly in heart, and you will find rest for your souls. For my yoke is easy, and my burden is light."

Missional: Take a few moments and reflect on the burdens in your life. Be still and know that the Lord wants to take them away. Pray and release your worries and burdens at the feet of Jesus.

Meditate: I pray you know you are *loved*, you are *worthy*, and you are *His*. You have a *purpose*, and He has a plan that is far greater than you could ask or imagine. He will complete it in and through *you*. Don't give up. Rest in Him today.

Heavenly Father,

Thank You for listening to my worries and concerns. I cast all my burdens onto You because You care for me. Your yoke is easy, and Your burden is light. I want to be still and let You fight my battles for me. I release all my burdens to You, O Lord.

In Jesus's name, Amen

YOUR DAILY WEAPON: THE ARMOR OF GOD

I want to encourage you today to be strong in the Lord and trust in His authority, power, and grace over your life.

Do you ever feel like you're in a constant battle with the world around you? A battle that oftentimes has you feeling defeated, with no strength to continue, and you want to just throw in the towel and give up? You know those circumstances that keep building upon themselves, getting deeper and heavier to bear in your own strength. The good news is there is a weapon you can use every day to strengthen and prepare you for any and every battle that comes your way: the armor of God.

Ephesians 6:10–12 tells us:

> Finally, be strong in the Lord and in his mighty power. Put on the full armor of God, so that you can take your stand against the devil's schemes. For our struggle is not against flesh and blood, but against the rulers, against the authorities, against the powers of this dark world and against the spiritual forces of evil in the heavenly realms.

This passage highlights the truth of spiritual warfare, compelling believers to be empowered by the Lord and His strength. It emphasizes that our fight is against spiritual wickedness, not human beings, and calls for us to put on the "armor of God" to oppose the devil's plans and stand firm against the forces of darkness, focusing on the nature of the conflict.

The enemy is strategic and cunning. He knows your patterns, and he uses those things to plan his attacks. He studies you. He knows your weaknesses and temptations. First Peter 5:8 says, "Be alert and of sober mind. Your enemy the devil prowls around like a roaring lion looking for someone to devour." This verse commands believers to maintain a watchful stance, refusing to be ignorant of the devil's ploys. Instead, you must actively oppose his attacks with a strong faith in God. This is a call to grow in spiritual discernment and remember that your struggles are common to all believers.

What does it mean to be strong in the Lord? Being strong in the Lord requires disciplines of faith. Prioritizing prayer daily cultivates an intimate relationship with the Lord. This will equip you to discern His voice from the other loud voices in your head. Studying His Word is necessary to understand the truth versus the lies of the enemy. The enemy twists and distorts the truth and repackages it to appear good. There is power in knowledge. Read your Bible daily. Let your heart blossom and have awareness of its dependence on God.

The armor of God is your equipment to prepare you for any attack from the enemy. Let's look at Ephesians 6:13–17:

Therefore put on the full armor of God, so that when the day of evil comes, you may be able to stand your ground, and after you have done everything, to stand. Stand firm then, with the belt of truth buckled around your waist, with the breastplate of righteousness in place, and with your feet fitted with the readiness that comes from the gospel of peace. In addition to all this, take up the shield of faith, with which you can extinguish all the flaming arrows of the evil one. Take the helmet of salvation and the sword of the Spirit, which is the word of God.

Paul clarifies in this passage that the believer's struggle is a genuine spiritual battle against evil forces, extending beyond mere human conflict. He therefore urges them to prepare by equipping themselves with God's armor. The armor is simple: You need a belt of truth—the Word of God; a breastplate of righteousness—living holy; feet fitted with readiness for the gospel of peace—preparation; a shield of faith—trust in God's promises; a helmet of salvation—God's saving grace; and the sword of the Spirit—the Word of God. These pieces of armor will equip you to stand firm against the devil's schemes.

Are you equipped to fight your battles? Do you have the full armor of God? I urge you to get equipped so you do not fall prey to the enemy's tactics. Remember, we do not fight flesh and blood. Humans are not our enemies. It is what is behind the scenes that you do not see that is working things out to seek, kill, and destroy you and God's purposes for your life.

The last piece of armor is the most important: prayer. Ephesians 6:18 says, "And pray in the Spirit on all occasions with all kinds of prayers and requests. With this in mind, be alert and always keep on praying for all the Lord's people." This verse emphasizes praying constantly, fervently, and in the Spirit for every possible need and situation, while also being watchful and persistently praying for all believers. Fervent prayer is a passionate, sincere, and earnest petition to God. Praying strategically with fervor, using God's Word, is a battlefield kind of prayer.

I have read many books on the armor of God and spiritual warfare. The first one that comes to mind is *Fervent Prayer* by Priscilla Shirer. *Fervent Prayer* is an empowering book that teaches you how to develop a powerful prayer life and overcome the enemy's attacks. I learned how to pray strategic prayers, and I remember writing them down and putting them on my prayer wall. I kept them up for years as a reminder that prayer is powerful.

MAKING IT ABOUT ME

Message: *Get ready for battle.* Read the following Scriptures and meditate on these truths for a while. Let them simmer in your spirit before moving on.

> Ephesians 6:10–12: "Finally, be strong in the Lord and in his mighty power. Put on the full armor of God, so that you can take your stand against the devil's schemes. For our struggle is not against flesh

and blood, but against the rulers, against the authorities, against the powers of this dark world and against the spiritual forces of evil in the heavenly realms."

1 Peter 5:8: "Be alert and of sober mind. Your enemy the devil prowls around like a roaring lion looking for someone to devour."

Ephesians 6:18: "And pray in the Spirit on all occasions with all kinds of prayers and requests. With this in mind, be alert and always keep on praying for all the Lord's people."

Missional: Take a few moments and reflect on your prayer life. How often do you pray? Do you pray strategically? Do you write your prayers down or keep a daily journal to see what prayers have been answered? Do you pray Gods Word back to Him? Take the next few lines and write a strategic prayer in an area of your life that is under attack. You can use the Scriptures from today to help you.

Meditate: My prayer for you today is to get equipped for battle. Put on the full armor of God. Draw near to God, and He will draw near to you. Be strong in the Lord.

Heavenly Father,

Thank You, Lord, for the armor of God that equips us to go to battle in the spiritual realms. Your Word is the sword of the Spirit and pierces and demolishes any stronghold or lie of the enemy. Equip me with Your Word, Lord, and help me meditate on Your promises day and night. May the words of my mouth and the meditation of my heart be pleasing in Your sight, Lord, my Rock and my Redeemer.

In Jesus's name, Amen

ABANDONMENT

ABANDONMENT—SURRENDERING YOUR LIFE AND DEEPENING YOUR RELATIONSHIP WITH GOD.

Therefore, I urge you, brothers and sisters, in view of God's mercy, to offer your bodies as a living sacrifice, holy and pleasing to God—this is your true and proper worship.

ROMANS 12:1

A life surrendered to God's will is our spiritual act of worship and is holy and pleasing to God. We are empty vessels waiting to be filled with the Holy Spirit to live life abundantly in the presence of the Lord. We must surrender our will and expectations, allowing the Holy Spirit to guide us into all truth, leading us to our kingdom purpose. We must let go of the things of this world and focus our eyes on things above, dwelling in Him richly to bring heaven here on earth. Our absolute surrender brings a transformed life and leads us to serve and bless those around us. We get to participate in the stories bringing life, light, and freedom to our circles of influence.

One of my favorite books that I read early on in my faith journey with the Lord is *Absolute Surrender* by Andrew Murray. It helped me understand how my life would be transformed by living surrendered to the Lord. This surrender would draw me deeper into a relationship with Jesus and lead me to my kingdom purpose. Andrew Murray writes:

This absolute surrender to God will wonderfully bless us … But do remember, there must be absolute surrender. At every tea-table you see it. Why is tea poured into that cup? Because it is empty and given up for the tea. But put ink, or vinegar, or wine into it, and will they pour the tea into the vessel? And can God fill you, can God bless you, if you are not absolutely surrendered to Him? He cannot. Let us believe God has wonderful blessings for us, if we will but stand up for God, and say, be it with a trembling will, yet with a believing heart: "O God, I accept thy demands. I am thine and all that I have."

Living a life surrendered to God's will and letting go of your efforts to try to control the outcome of life will lead you to a life lived with kingdom purpose.

THE BLESSED LIFE: SURRENDERING TO GOD'S WILL

I want to encourage you to surrender your will to the Lord. He has a plan and a purpose for your life. Trust in His provision for you.

Are you looking to the world to measure your standard of living? Do you find yourself wanting or chasing things that you believe will satisfy your desires and make you feel whole? Are you chasing dreams that you never seem to catch? Are you tired of living and conforming to what society or the culture deems a worthy and meaningful life? Do you feel like it never seems to bring lasting joy or purpose?

Living life for the world or for selfish desires will never bring lasting contentment or a fulfilling life. It will always keep you striving and wanting more.

Romans 12:1–2: "Therefore, I urge you, brothers and sisters, in view of God's mercy, to offer your bodies as a living sacrifice, holy and pleasing to God—this is your true and proper worship. Do not conform to the pattern of this world, but be transformed by the renewing of your mind. Then you will be able to test and approve what God's will is—his good, pleasing and perfect will." This passage urges believers to dedicate their lives to God as a "living sacrifice." It's not a one-time decision but a daily process of letting God transform your mind so you can understand and follow His will.

This is a continuous sacrifice that takes dedication and prayer. You must let go of your fleshly desires and allow the Holy Spirit to renew your mind daily. As your relationship with the Lord deepens, it will be easier to discern the will of God. If you are not living a life that is honoring to God or making decisions that align with God's Word, you are not living in the will of God. If your decisions go against the truth, then you are not living in obedience and you are not aligning with God's purposes for you. You must surrender your will to the Lord and walk in obedience to discern God's good and perfect will for your life.

Jesus tells us in Matthew 10:39, "Whoever finds their life will lose it, and whoever loses their life for my sake will find it." It is a metaphor for surrendering your will, desires, and ambitions to follow Jesus. Worldly pursuits lead to spiritual loss, while kingdom pursuits lead to a true life. Having a kingdom mindset will lead you to a purposeful and fulfilling life with an eternal perspective.

Psalm 37:5–6 says, "Commit your way to the LORD; trust in him and he will do this: He will make your righteous reward shine like the dawn." The verse encourages believers to surrender control of their lives to the Lord and place their full confidence in Him, thereby inviting His divine intervention. Surrendering your will, letting go of your selfish ambition, walking in faith, and trusting God will bring divine authority over your life.

I lived most of my life for selfish gain, pursuing the things of this world in the hope that I would gain happiness and lasting peace. I was always trying to be a better version of myself. I wanted validation and acceptance from my peers and the world around me. Nothing I did ever changed my internal struggle to achieve outward perfection. It never will, if I am looking to the world for my acceptance. I prayed Romans 12:1 over my life many years ago after having a divine intervention with the Lord. My heart saw the light, and I no longer wanted what this world had to offer. I started viewing life differently. I had an eternal perspective in every circumstance and every decision I made. I wanted to live my life for Jesus, giving Him all the glory. I pray daily and ask the Lord to give me His eyes to see others and myself the way He does. It is a daily sacrifice and takes dedication and devotion to the Lord.

Our lives are just a vapor when you look at it from an eternal perspective.

We are given the gift of life each day we wake up. How we choose to live matters and can have a positive impact on others if we live for kingdom purposes. A life surrendered to the will of God is a blessed life—a life that has deep meaning and true fulfillment.

MAKING IT ABOUT ME

Message: *A blessed life is a life surrendered to God's will.* Read the following Scriptures and meditate on these truths for a while. Let them simmer in your spirit before moving on.

> Romans 12:1–2: "Therefore, I urge you, brothers and sisters, in view of God's mercy, to offer your bodies as a living sacrifice, holy and pleasing to God—this is your true and proper worship. Do not conform to the pattern of this world but be transformed by the renewing of your mind. Then you will be able to test and approve what God's will is—his good, pleasing and perfect will."

> Psalm 37:5–6: "Commit your way to the LORD; trust in him and he will do this: He will make your righteous reward shine like the dawn."

> Matthew 10:39: "Whoever finds their life will lose it, and whoever loses their life for my sake will find it."

Missional: Take a few moments and reflect on the areas of your life that you struggle to surrender to God. What fears or doubts hinder your surrender, and how can you cultivate a deeper trust in God's plan for you? How can you develop a stronger relationship with the Lord so you can better discern His will?

Meditate: I pray you surrender your will to God and seek the things that bring lasting joy and contentment. Let go and trust in the Lord. He has a blessed and beautiful plan for your life.

Heavenly Father,

Thank You for Your provisions in my life. I know the plans You have for me, and they are better than the plans I have for myself. I surrender my will to You and trust in Your promises. Your love is steadfast and true.

In Jesus's name, Amen

REPLACING FEAR WITH FAITH: A PATH TO FREEDOM

I want to encourage you today to focus on faith and God's promises over any fear or anxiousness that may try to settle into your heart. Let God's truth resonates and illuminate your spirit today.

Do you tend to have a fear of something that gets in the way of your daily life? Do you get anxious when you have no root cause, especially in the moment when the feeling of panic overtakes your body? Do you let your fears stop you from living and take the joy out of your day? In the moment of sudden difficulties, do you focus most of your attention on the fear rather than the truth of God's Word? Do you give your worry to God, or do you marinate in it?

I know that in my own life I have struggled with many fears, some rational and many irrational. While rational fears serve as a response to actual risks, exemplified by the fear of falling from a cliff, irrational fears can escalate into phobias. These phobias are characterized by intense anxiety that disrupts everyday life, even when the feared object or situation poses no genuine danger. According to Neil Anderson, there are three types of fear: the fear of people, the fear of failure, and the fear of death. Every fear falls into one of these categories. Neil Anderson's book *Freedom from Fear* centers on the idea that faith empowers individuals to overcome irrational fears by actively acknowledging and renouncing them, rather than suppressing them. *Freedom from Fear* helped me gain a deeper understanding of fear, worry, and anxiety and gave me tools and strategies to combat the battle in my mind. I highly recommend this book if you struggle with any of these emotional strongholds.

For most of my life I struggled with the fear of death. It had a grip on me. Many of my irrational fears stemmed from this one fear. I was exposed to a very powerful movie at age nine that dealt with demonic possession. I was told that this was real, and it haunted me into adulthood. I had an irrational fear because I didn't know the truth of God's Word and the depths of the gospel. I didn't realize that the fear of Satan was a powerful stronghold over my life, and I was believing his lies. My fear of death stemmed from the enemy's lies and torment over my soul. It led me to have so many irrational fears. I was able to break free and live a life that is focused on a faith object—Jesus—rather than a fear object—death. After breaking free from the bondage of fear, I no longer have a fear of death. I know death has no sting, and I am a child of God. I replaced the lie with truth. This strategy can be used with anything that is opposed to God's Word.

Second Timothy 1:7 (NKJV) tells us: "For God has not given us a spirit of fear, but of power and of love and of a sound mind."

Paul writes to Timothy not only to encourage him but also to contrast the paralysis of fear with the empowering grace of God, which enables a life of boldness and love even in difficult times. He reminds Timothy and all believers that instead of fear, they should rely on the Holy Spirit's power, love, and sound judgment to guide them.

If you struggle with worry, fear, or anxiety, draw near to God, and He will draw near to you. Rest in His goodness and presence. First Peter 5:7 tells us, "Cast all your anxiety on him because he cares for you." Fear is a liar.

MAKING IT ABOUT ME

Message: *You have a spirit of power and a sound mind.* Read the following Scriptures and meditate on these truths for a while. Let them simmer in your spirit before moving on.

2 Timothy 1:7 (NKJV): "For God has not given us a spirit of fear, but of power and of love and of a sound mind."

1 Peter 5:7: "Cast all your anxiety on him because he cares for you."

Missional: Take a few moments and reflect on God's unwavering character and promises that help you overcome fear and find peace. What are some of the common lies that anxiety whispers to you, and how can you counter them with God's truth?

Meditate: I pray that you focus on faith and God's promises today and know that you have a spirit of power and that fear is a liar.

Heavenly Father,

Thank You for giving me the peace that surpasses all understanding amid the anxiety and fears that whisper lies to me. I cast all my fears onto You because You care for me. You are my refuge and my strength in times of despair.

In Jesus's name, Amen

"IT IS FINISHED": THE FOUNDATION OF GRACE

I want to encourage you today to fully let go of the continued striving that easily entangles you and leads to burnout, leaving you with a weary soul. You know that His grace is enough and that you do not have to keep behaving a certain way to please God. Your behavior doesn't determine the depths of God's grace toward you. Your behavior will never change how much God loves you once you belong to the kingdom of God. God's wrath no longer applies to you, the believer. You were saved by grace and grace alone once you trusted Jesus as your Lord and Savior. Nothing you do will ever change that kind of love—a sacrificial love that was nailed to the cross for you.

Do you try to earn grace? Is your primary motivation for doing good works out of duty or obligation to God? Do you strive to earn favor by continually judging another person's sinful behavior so God will be pleased with you? Are your good deeds stemming from a grateful heart or a guilty one? Are you letting grace lead you to a life that is lived abundantly in Christ?

In John 19:30, Jesus's final words on the cross, "It is finished" (*tetelestai* in Greek), signified the end of His earthly mission and the complete atonement for sin through His sacrificial death, bringing about redemption. This is our declaration of faith. Jesus bore our sin and paid the penalty for us. He extended mercy—not giving us what we deserved: death. Jesus spoke these famous last words as He endured the excruciating pain and suffering crucifixion brought unto Him, allowing the sinner to be pardoned. This pardon is granted when we repent of our sins, ask for forgiveness, and place our trust in Jesus.

Ephesians 2:8–9 says: "For it is by grace you have been saved, through faith—and this is not from yourselves, it is the gift of God—not by works, so that no one can boast." Salvation comes to you through grace, and it is received by faith. This is not something you produced; it is God's gracious gift. Therefore, no one has grounds for boasting. There is nothing greater than this grace, a grace freely lavished on the believer.

Once you believed and put your trust in Jesus, you were given something you did not deserve: the gift of salvation by grace alone.

How do you allow grace to overflow in your life without letting self-righteousness impede your decisions and actions? How do we confess and repent of our sins with lasting freedom? Romans 3:23 says, "For all have sinned and fall short of the glory of God." This verse stresses that sin is not limited by social standing or personal conduct; everyone falls short of God's righteousness. We are sinful by nature, but Jesus imputes His righteousness upon us when we are saved. The Holy Spirit teaches us and guides us in all truth. This involves growing in holiness and separating from sin. It is a lifelong process called sanctification. Conviction allows us to discern and turn from sin and unholiness. There is no condemnation in Christ Jesus (Rom. 8:1), but when we live out of gratitude and thankfulness for what was given to us—redemption—we are more inclined to walk in freedom and turn from our sin.

I can honestly say that grace was a hard concept to grasp when I started my faith journey with the Lord. I grew up with a misconception of how God loves. I related to God and His character based on the relationship I had as a child with my earthly father. I did not understand what unconditional love meant. I thought my behavior determined the love I would receive from my dad. If I obeyed and did all the right things, I would receive love, but if I made a mistake, then the reaction or consequences were never handled with grace and mercy. These internal struggles as a child led me to become a rule follower and ultimately self-righteous. I thought of God as a dictator, and I felt I was never going to live up to His standards. This led me down some dark paths, which eventually led me on a journey seeking truth. Jesus pursued me, and in the long run, my eyes saw the light and learned the goodness of mercy and grace.

MAKING IT ABOUT ME

Message: *Jesus offers us a sacrificial kind of love.* Read the following Scriptures and meditate on these truths for a while. Let them simmer in your spirit before moving on.

> Ephesians 2:8–9: "For it is by grace you have been saved, through faith—and this is not from yourselves, it is the gift of God—not by works, so that no one can boast."
>
> Romans 3:23: "For all have sinned and fall short of the glory of God."
>
> John 19:30: "It is finished."

Missional: Take a few moments and reflect on the love and sacrifice Jesus bore for you and the grace that was given to you at salvation. Write down three people you can extend grace and love to today.

Meditate: I pray the goodness and sacrificial love of Jesus draws you near today and captivates your soul. You are a chosen child of the Most High King. Let His grace be enough for you today.

Heavenly Father,

Thank You for the gift of salvation and Your love extended at the cross that covers all my sins. Help me extend this grace and love to others in my life. You are my stronghold and my strong tower. It is finished!

In Jesus's name, Amen

THE CALL TO AGAPE: LOVING LIKE JESUS

I want to encourage you today to continue loving and sacrificing your needs for your spouse, your children, your parents, your siblings, your friends, and your neighbors. Be the good in someone's day. Shine your light for all to see. Love like Jesus.

Are you able to love a person no matter the cost? Can you see past another person's faults and continue to love them with all your heart? Do you have a motive for giving your love to another? Do you demand or expect to receive something in return when you do something for someone else? Is your love conditional? Do you have the capacity to love your enemies well? Are you loving sacrificially?

You were created for a divine purpose, a purpose that only you can fulfill. You were created by God with a unique design, and you were given all your treasures, gifts, and talents the day you were born. The journey of life is to pursue your purpose and live on mission for the kingdom of God. Jesus says in Matthew 22:37, "Love the Lord your God with all your heart and with all your soul and with all your mind." Jesus then goes on to say that the second greatest commandment is to "love your neighbor as yourself." The questions to ask yourself and let your heart ruminate on are these: Do I love God with my whole heart? Do I desire to know Him intimately? Does the Lord occupy the deepest crevices of my mind? Do I love others the same way?

First and foremost, we must love God with our whole heart and love our neighbors well to truly walk in our divine purpose and destiny. We will live life abundantly, with a transformed heart and a God-driven outcome. Mark 10:45 says, "For even the Son of Man did not come to be served, but to serve, and to give his life as a ransom for many." The core message of Mark 10:45 is that greatness lies in service and self-sacrifice, urging Jesus's followers to imitate His humility.

Jesus is the epitome of how we should live our lives—a life of service to those around us, including those people that are hard to love. They need us the most. They are craving to be loved, and we are called to love completely and sacrificially to participate in the stories of those around us. We have the divine opportunity to bring light, life, and freedom into dark spaces, bringing redemption and transformation to those troubled hearts. This is a call that requires self-sacrifice and a desire to live on mission for the kingdom of God.

A call to love well is not easy, especially when we struggle to love ourselves. Loving out of humility rather than obligation or position is a challenge for all of us. We all know clichés about love like "love is blind," "love conquers all," "love is love," "love at first sight," "love means never saying you're sorry," and my favorite, "you complete me." These all stem from a surface knowledge of love, love that fulfills a need that gives us temporal satisfaction. It invites the question: Do we really know what love is? How can we love sacrificially and deeply if we lack the knowledge of what true love means? True love can be defined only by the character of God.

How does God define love? First John 4:8 tells us, "Whoever does not love does not know God, because God is love." God is love but not love by a worldly definition or standard. It is deeper; it is called *agape*.

What is an agape kind of love?

Britannica defines *agape* as this: "In the New Testament, the fatherly love of God for humans, as well as the human reciprocal love for God. In Scripture, the transcendent agape love is the highest form of love and is contrasted with eros, or erotic love, and philia, or brotherly love. In John 3:16, a verse that is often described as a summary of the Gospel message, agape is the word used for the love that moved God to send his only son for the world's redemption."

This is a love that transcends all understanding, a love defined by God, a love that is sacrificial in nature and requires humility.

According to the Bible Project, agape love transcends mere emotion; rather, it's a conscious decision to act in ways that foster the well-being of others. This love is characterized by its unconditional and sacrificial nature, mirroring God's love for humanity despite their imperfections. Furthermore, believers are called to extend this same agape love to one another, following the example set by Jesus's love for His followers. We are called to love on a different level as Christ followers.

Loving a person unconditionally is difficult, but we can do this if we choose to let go of our expectations and selfish ambition. We can look at our relational dynamics and discover where we need to love and allow ourselves to surrender and lay our life down for another, like Jesus did for us.

Marriage is a covenant with God and requires sacrificial work for the man and the woman to be one with God—a good depiction of our relationship with Christ. Matthew 19:6 says, "So they are no longer two, but one flesh. Therefore what God has joined together, let no one separate." At its heart, this verse articulates the Christian view of marriage as a lasting and unified relationship between a husband and wife.

I have been with my husband for almost forty years. We have built a wonderful life together. I can tell you that there have been many beautiful and challenging seasons on this journey of love. We are both flawed and broken vessels that have our own walk with God. We are continually being refined and changed into the image and character of God. It is a process, and it takes disciplines of the faith to renew our minds and bring the unity of Christ within the center of our marriage. I was asked recently by a friend, "What is the secret to longevity in your marriage?" The simple answer is to love each other the way we love Jesus—to give up our desires and needs no matter the cost, to surrender our will even when we know we are right, and to let humility drive us, not pride. We don't always get this right, but we continue to love and work on our marriage daily. The intimacy and relationship I have with my husband has evolved over the years. I can recognize his voice in a crowded room, and with just one look, I know what he is saying to me without words. I know his desires, his weaknesses, and his strengths. I have a deeper understanding of his motivation and desires in life. I seek to bring the best out of him, and I long to love and serve him well. My relationship with him mirrors my relationship with Jesus. We can be still with each other in silence and are both content. We have a deep, sacrificial kind of love—agape.

MAKING IT ABOUT ME

Message: *Love others like Jesus first loved you.* Read the following Scriptures and meditate on these truths for a while. Let them simmer in your spirit before moving on.

> Matthew 22:37: "Love the Lord your God with all your heart and with all your soul and with all your mind."

> Mark 10:45: "For even the Son of Man did not come to be served, but to serve, and to give his life as a ransom for many."

> 1 John 4:8: "Whoever does not love does not know God, because God is love."

> Matthew 19:6: "So they are no longer two, but one flesh. Therefore what God has joined together, let no one separate."

Missional: Take a few moments and reflect on how you love others. Do you love those around you with unconditional love? Do you love the Lord with all your heart? Write down three ways you can show sacrificial love to someone today.

Meditate: I pray you have a desire to love the people around you well and seek your divine purpose—living sacrificially, giving yourself to your inner circle and beyond, loving God and your neighbor as yourself.

Heavenly Father,

Thank You for loving me when I did not even love myself. You are a true example of sacrificial love. Help me love those around me unconditionally, sacrificing my time and energy for someone else. You are faithful and true.

In Jesus's name, Amen

LETTING GO: FINDING HEALING THROUGH FORGIVENESS

I want to encourage you today to let go of the grudge or the hurt someone caused you, no matter how difficult the pain. Let humility take the place of pride in your heart. Release it to God. Let God work it out in the other person's heart. Forgive anyway.

How do you forgive? Are you quick to forgive if you know you are wrong, or do you hold on to your pride and convince yourself the other person was at fault? Do you take offense against the other person if they do not apologize? Do you apologize easily even if you are right, then still hold the pain in and let their offenses continue to hurt you? Do you forgive yourself easily? Do you allow others to determine how you are feeling based on their actions or lack of action toward you? Do you put high expectations on others, expecting some fairy-tale outcome? When your expectations fall short and do not align with your false sense of reality, do you get upset? Do you hold on to unforgiveness in your heart? These questions illustrate many of the struggles I had to work through in my own life with many different relational dynamics. It is not easy, but there is freedom in forgiveness.

Let's look at the life of Jesus. John 1:1 tells us, "In the beginning was the Word, and the Word was with God, and the Word was God." According to this verse, the Word existed prior to creation and was with God initially. Further,

John 1:14 says, "The Word became flesh and made his dwelling among us. We have seen his glory, the glory of the one and only Son, who came from the Father, full of grace and truth." The divine Word of God, Jesus, became human and dwelt among us. His life and teachings manifested God's glory, a glory that goes beyond mere physical splendor to reveal God's grace and truth, offered to everyone who believes.

Imagine the love the Father has for His children to give us His one and only Son, Jesus, to live among us in the flesh, to dwell with humanity and all the brutality that goes with being human in this world. The sacrificial and righteous love that was imputed upon us. Jesus lived a perfect life and yet was mocked, treated unjustly, subjected to many false accusations, and left alone when things got difficult by those who were closest to Him. Yet He did not sin or treat anyone with anger or malice. He loved like the Father. Jesus paid the penalty we all deserved. He humbled Himself. Philippians 2:8 says, "And being found in appearance as a man, he humbled himself by becoming obedient to death—even death on a cross!"

His death demonstrated the depths of His humility, obedience, and self-sacrifice for us. Jesus bore the punishment of our sinful nature. He made amends for our offenses and wrongdoing by dying on the cross and bearing the weight of our sin—the ultimate act of forgiveness, atonement. Luke 23:34 (ESV) records Jesus's prayer on the cross, "Father, forgive them, for they know not what they do." Jesus was forgiving us even though our sin was the reason He suffered.

In the Old Testament, the prophet Isaiah foretold the pain and suffering that would be endured by Jesus. Isaiah 53:4–5 says, "Surely he took up our pain and bore our suffering, yet we considered him punished by God, stricken by him, and afflicted. But he was pierced for our transgressions, he was crushed for our iniquities; the punishment that brought us peace was on him, and by his wounds we are healed."

The love and sacrifice of letting go of our selfishness and our prideful hearts will lead you and me to forgive and let go of the pain, no matter how deep or how wounded we are from the offense. Once you forgive and give it to

God, you are set free—free to love and even make amends within your own heart, and eventually love will replace the hurt. Let God do the work of restoration and redemption in the other person's heart.

I have walked through many offenses that caused me pain and even long-term suffering. Some relationships were harder to forgive than others. I believe the closer the person, the more difficult it is to forgive and release the hurt. I have held grudges and played the blame game. I grumbled and had many internal struggles to let the hurt go. I am not going to lie and say this process is easy, but once I forgave myself and released the burdens at the feet of Jesus, I was able to deeply forgive the offender. Once I surrendered my hurt to the Lord, I was able to love that person again with my whole heart. Some of those relationships are completely mended, and others are not meant for me to pursue and redeem. But my hurt and offense toward them are nailed to the cross—completely forgiven!

I read a book called *Bait of Satan* by John Bevere many years ago that helped me tremendously. I was in a season of grumbling that led me to keep an offense against a few people in my life. This book was timely. I learned how to not only forgive my offenders but also to pray for them. It was such a healing transformation in my heart. It changed how I relate to my offenders today.

MAKING IT ABOUT ME

Message: *Let humility take its place in your heart and forgive.* Read the following Scriptures and meditate on these truths for a while. Let them simmer in your spirit before moving on.

John 1:1: "In the beginning was the Word, and the Word was with God, and the Word was God."

John 1:14: "The Word became flesh and made his dwelling among us. We have seen his glory, the glory of the one and only Son, who came from the Father, full of grace and truth."

Philippians 2:8: "And being found in appearance as a man, he humbled himself by becoming obedient to death—even death on a cross!"

Luke 23:34 (ESV): "Father, forgive them, for they know not what they do."

Isaiah 53:4–5: "Surely he took up our pain and bore our suffering, yet we considered him punished by God, stricken by him, and afflicted. But he was pierced for our transgressions, he was crushed for our iniquities; the punishment that brought us peace was on him, and by his wounds we are healed."

Missional: Take a few moments and reflect on any unforgiveness stirring in your heart that you need to give to God. Write down those that you need to forgive and surrender the offenders in your life to God.

Meditate: I pray that you find forgiveness in your heart for the offenders in your life. Don't let the pain cause you to harden your heart. Release it to Jesus. You will be transformed and set free from the burden of the offense.

Heavenly Father,

Thank You for forgiving me and giving me grace upon grace. I want to extend forgiveness to my offenders and give them grace. You teach us to forgive seven times seventy. You are a God of humanity and goodness.

In Jesus's name, Amen

PRAYER AND PROVISION: ALIGNING YOUR LIFE WITH GOD'S WILL

I want to encourage you to pray and bring God's provisions in your life to fruition. Spend time with the Lord and surrender to His will. Prayer opens up communication with the Lord. Come to the throne of grace with a thankful heart today.

Do you feel that your prayers are not being heard by God? Do you struggle to open up to the Lord with all of your heart? Including the deep parts of your soul, the parts you try to hide? Is your prayer life dry or nonexistent? Do you find yourself struggling to pray longer than a minute? Maybe you are not sure how to communicate with God. Maybe saying a quick prayer in the morning, a blessing before dinner, and a quick prayer in the evening before bed is all you know because that was what you were taught as a child. Those prayers typically ask God to bless you and your family. We are all guilty of those types of prayers in our lives. Using God like a genie in a bottle. Asking God for prayers to be granted the way we want them answered. You know, our will be done, not His. Is prayer a means to an end in your life, a box to check off in your daily life as a Christian? Do you spend time talking and listening to God? Do you give God more of your time than you do other activities in your life? Is prayer a tool to use, or a conversation with God?

The power of prayer brings divine intervention into our circumstances through faith The definition of *prayer* according to Dictionary.com is a solemn request for help or expression of thanks addressed to God or an object of worship, or the act or practice of praying to God or an object of worship. Jesus is the object of faith that opens the door to the Father in prayer. The Bible uses the word *prayer* or a variation of the word a total of 375 times, according to the *NIV Exhaustive Concordance*. Prayer is an open communication with the Lord. It is a way for us to express our gratitude, needs, and desires and to draw closer to Him.

Jeremiah 29:12 tells us: "Then you will call on me and come and pray to me, and I will listen to you." This verse emphasizes the Lord's promise to hear and respond to His people when they call upon Him in prayer.

First Thessalonians 5:17 (ESV) says, "Pray without ceasing." This verse doesn't mean to constantly pray without stopping all day long. Instead, it emphasizes consistent communication with God, a position of dependence, and a inclination to turn to Him in prayer throughout all circumstances. We should pray with a humble heart with gratitude and thanksgiving, knowing God will work everything out for our good.

Mark 11:24 says, "Therefore I tell you, whatever you ask for in prayer, believe that you have received it, and it will be yours." The power of our faith lies in prayer. This doesn't mean that God will answer all prayers the way you see fit if you just have enough faith or pray harder. It has to align with God's will for your life. An unanswered prayer is really an answered prayer. God knows best.

Psalm 100:4 says, "Enter his gates with thanksgiving and his courts with praise; give thanks to him and praise his name," and Colossians 3:17 tells us, "And whatever you do, whether in word or deed, do it all in the name of the Lord Jesus, giving thanks to God the Father through him." The Lord is worthy of our time, praise, and worship. Prayer opens the point of contact for provision and the will of God. Prayer is the process used by God that releases what He intends to do in your life. God knows His plans for you, even if you don't. It is not a surprise to Him. Your life has meaning and purpose that God has predestined for you before you were born. Living in His will unlocks the power, and prayer opens the door to your kingdom purposes. Prayer does not make God do what He never planned to do in your life. But prayer releases the edict of what God had already planned to do to bring you to your kingdom purpose. God releases your provisions if it is in His will to do so.

I can attest to the power of prayer in my life and the lives of those dear to me. Prayer has been the place that I have felt the presence of the Lord very tangibly in my life. I have seen the Lord work miracles in my life and the lives around me through circled and fervent prayers. I have circled the same prayers over my life and my family's lives, sometimes for many years without a breakthrough, and witnessed God move in ways only He could. Sometimes I can think about something I want or need, and God answers my thought without me even asking. Those are some of my favorite moments with Him. I have cried and fervently prayed for an answer, and God was silent and my prayers were unanswered. I have learned in these seasons of drought to trust in the Lord's sovereignty and praise Him in the waiting. There is an answer to every prayer. His will in our lives will be done, bringing us to our kingdom purpose.

MAKING IT ABOUT ME

Message: *Prayer and provision align you with God's will.* Read the following Scriptures and meditate on these truths for a while. Let them simmer in your spirit before moving on.

Jeremiah 29:12: "Then you will call on me and come and pray to me, and I will listen to you."

1 Thessalonians 5:17 (esv): "Pray without ceasing."

Mark 11:24: "Therefore I tell you, whatever you ask for in prayer, believe that you have received it, and it will be yours."

Psalm 100:4: "Enter his gates with thanksgiving and his courts with praise; give thanks to him and praise his name."

Colossians 3:17: "And whatever you do, whether in word or deed, do it all in the name of the Lord Jesus, giving thanks to God the Father through him."

Missional: Take a few moments and reflect on what you are grateful for today. What keeps you from prayer? How can you set aside time for prayer on a daily basis? How can you incorporate prayer throughout your day?

Meditate: I pray you spend time with the Lord giving Him your whole heart. His provisions are good, and His will for your life is perfect.

Heavenly Father,

Thank You for all the blessings in my life. The blessings I see and the many blessings I don't see. I know You are working them all out for my good and Your glory. Draw near to me and help me align my will with Yours. You are my defender and provision.

In Jesus's name, Amen

THE POWER OF MERCY: REFLECTING GOD'S LOVE IN A BROKEN WORLD

I want to encourage you to be kind to those around you. You do not know what they are going through. Everyone has a story God is writing. We do not know what chapter is unfolding before us. We get the privilege to be a part of people's stories and participate with the Lord in bringing grace and redemption in the lives of those in our circles of influence.

Are you someone that shies away from people who do not share your beliefs? Do you have an attitude of judgment toward others that do not follow your standards? Do you judge others by God's truth with love, kindness, and respect, or by the worldly standards of our cultural norms in society with an attitude of self-righteousness? Do you show mercy over judgment?

James 2:13 tells us, "Because judgment without mercy will be shown to anyone who has not been merciful. Mercy triumphs over judgment." This verse emphasizes God's harsh judgment on those that do not show mercy to others. You will face unmerciful judgment from God. When you extend mercy and positive acts of grace upon others, you will experience God's mercy and grace in your life. Matthew 7:1–2 also tells us: "Do not judge, or you too will be judged. For in the same way you judge others, you will be judged, and with the measure you use, it will be measured to you." Jesus tells His followers to avoid judging others harshly, because they will be judged with the same measure they use. This isn't a precept instructing us to ignore wrongdoing but rather to refrain from being overly critical or condemning. People should concentrate on their own imperfections and aim to be understanding and kind when gauging others. We must judge the distinction between truth and error. We must judge biblically with responsibility and always lovingly. How do we walk alongside others without coming across as judgmental or seeming self-righteous or condemning if we do not share the same beliefs?

First Peter 4:8 says, "Above all, love each other deeply, because love covers over a multitude of sins." This verse encourages believers to cultivate a love that is heartfelt, compassionate, and forgiving toward others. God's character is love, but that is only one of His many attributes. As believers, we are called to love others in truth. Truth and love go hand in hand. The Word of God is our barometer for how we are called to live our lives.

As believers, we must uphold God's standards. God does not meet our standards. Leave the judgment and wrath to God when faced with conflict or unrighteousness.

We are born sinners and are inherently not good. This stems from the fall in the garden of Eden. Jesus is our righteousness, and He took on the wrath of God in the place of those that put their trust in Him. We were shown mercy and given grace. Let's extend that mercy and goodness to others. Jesus demonstrated the ultimate act of sacrificial kindness. This act of love leads others to repentance in God's perfect timing.

MAKING IT ABOUT ME

Message: *The power of mercy over judgment.* Read the following Scriptures and meditate on these truths for a while. Let them simmer in your spirit before moving on.

> James 2:13: "Because judgment without mercy will be shown to anyone who has not been merciful. Mercy triumphs over judgment."

Matthew 7:1–2: "Do not judge, or you too will be judged. For in the same way you judge others, you will be judged, and with the measure you use, it will be measured to you."

1 Peter 4:8: "Above all, love each other deeply, because love covers over a multitude of sins."

Missional: Take a few moments and reflect on how you can extend mercy and grace to those in your circle of influence who do not have the same beliefs. How does understanding God's mercy influence your perspective on your life and the lives of others? How can you live out walking in mercy over judgment?

Meditate: I pray you extend kindness to the world around you through love and truth. Love out of gratitude for what Jesus suffered on your behalf.

Heavenly Father,

Thank You for Your mercy and grace You extend to me every day. Help me love those around me well. I want to see others through Your eyes. Your steadfast love endures forever.

In Jesus's name, Amen

ADORATION

ADORATION—LIVING YOUR LIFE
CAPTIVATED BY JESUS AND LOVING
OTHERS FROM A THANKFUL HEART.

This is my commandment, that you love one another
as I have loved you. Greater love has no one than
this, that someone lay down his life for his friends.

JOHN 15:12–13 (ESV)

The biblical definition of *adoration* is praising God for who God is. Having a deep love and respect for the Lord will lead your heart to love and serve the world around you. Your life lived captivated by what God has done for you should overflow in all you say and do, leading you to a life of service. When you serve others in areas you struggle with in your own life, it will activate blessings and deepen your faith. You will begin to see redemption in those areas. You will see the overflow of grace in your life and the lives around you. The quote from Ann Voskamp, "Everything that matters in living comes down to giving," highlights the central role of generosity and selflessness in a fulfilling life. A life found when you have a deep adoration for Jesus. A life lived in adoration for Jesus will lead you to your purpose as you serve the world around you using your time, treasures, and talents.

CALLED TO SHINE: LIVING AS AN AMBASSADOR FOR CHRIST

I want to encourage you today to live life to its fullest and live like an ambassador for Christ. Enjoy every moment today as if it may be your last. Love those around you well. Spend a little more time doing something you love. Take a leap of faith and trust Jesus in the process. Let the Lord guide your steps as you walk with Him. Don't get caught up in the world or the busyness of the day. Take time to pray and be still with God. Bless and encourage those in your inner circle and those you encounter daily. Sprinkle joy and goodness as you move through each day. Encourage and love your neighbors well.

I know this can be difficult since every day has its setbacks, disappointments, and challenges. We can't always feel like spreading kindness and joy when things don't seem to be going our way and our circumstances are beyond our control. Then there are times when people tend to find it hard to love, and we give up before we even get started. We can easily get caught up in our daily grind, and we can forget to take the time to listen to and engage with the people around us. Oftentimes, we can let our views and beliefs dictate how we feel toward others without getting to know them.

Do you get frustrated with people easily? Do you tell yourself, *I am just not a people person*? Do you find that when others don't share your views or belief system, you get annoyed or even angry at them for not agreeing with your point of view? Are you someone who shies away from conversations that don't align with your views or beliefs for fear of offending that person? Or are you someone who must get your point across no matter the cost? Are you living a life that is based on what the world believes or how it says you should live, or are you living the way God intended for you to live? Are you living with a worldly mindset or a kingdom of God mindset?

Let's look at the story of apostle Paul, who was also known as Saul. Saul was a Jewish Pharisee and a Roman citizen born in Tarsus. He actively persecuted early followers of Jesus, even seeking to arrest them. He was on the road to Damascus when he had an encounter with Jesus. Acts 9:3–4 says, "As he neared Damascus on his journey, suddenly a light from heaven flashed around him. He fell to the ground and heard a voice say to him, 'Saul, Saul, why do you persecute me?'" How many times have we persecuted Jesus without even realizing it? We thought we were living a life for God, but in reality, we had the wrong belief system. We were persecuting others for the wrong reasons. Our way, our beliefs, our views were our own, not those of Jesus.

In Acts 9:5–16, we learn that Jesus brings Saul to a house on Straight Street, and the Lord calls to a man named Ananias in a vision. Jesus tells him to go to Saul and place his hands on him to restore his sight. Now, can you imagine the fear and trepidation in Ananias? He is called by Jesus to go to a person who is violently persecuting the followers of Jesus. Ananias was obedient to His call and went. Acts 9:17–19 says: "Then Ananias went to the house and entered it. Placing his hands on Saul, he said, 'Brother Saul, the Lord—Jesus, who appeared to you on the road as you were coming here—has sent me so that you may see again and be filled with the Holy Spirit.' Immediately, something like scales fell from Saul's eyes, and he could see again. He got up and was baptized, and after taking some food, he regained his strength." Through grace, Ananias led Saul to shed his incorrect beliefs and welcome Jesus into his life. Though not always easy, obedience is very likely the most direct way forward and the most evident way to honor God.

Imagine if we were all obedient to our call from God, living life for others no matter the cost, stepping into the lives of people bringing life, light, and freedom the way Ananias did. We would be living lives with purpose and abundance in Christ. We would live with passion for what we believe and would be living on mission for the kingdom of God. Once Saul was touched by Jesus, he was forever changed. He suffered for the cause of Christ. He was willing to endure hardships for living out his calling—bringing the gospel to the gentiles. He no longer went by his Hebrew name, Saul. After his conversion, he was known by his Roman name, Paul. He was living out his purpose with freedom in Christ. He was living life abundantly, on mission for the kingdom of God.

Are you living like Saul or Paul today?

Second Corinthians 5:17 says, "Therefore, if anyone is in Christ, the new creation has come: The old has gone, the new is here!" Once we are in Christ, we are made new, resulting in a fundamentally changed life and a new sense of self, bringing about a radical transformation and a new identity. Like Paul, we are made new once we have been touched and changed by Jesus. We have a choice: We can walk in the patterns and ways of this world, easily losing sight of our call, or we can walk in the Spirit every day and live out our purpose on mission for the kingdom of God.

I was once just like Saul, living with a wrong view of God. I made up my own cuddly god, a loving god that fit with my own agenda and beliefs. I believed in God and prayed, but I was living for me. I was selfish and did not understand the depths of the gospel. I didn't understand the grace that was given to me through the death and resurrection of Jesus. I was living a life that was self-righteous. I, like Paul, was touched by Jesus—a radical moment in my life that changed how I live today. I know that His grace is enough. I now live my life with a kingdom perspective, a life sacrificed for the people around me. My faith drives me to serve and love like Jesus, not because I must but because I get to. I get to participate in kingdom change for a God that pursued me and loved me first. I live as an ambassador for Christ, pursuing and walking in my kingdom purpose and destiny.

MAKING IT ABOUT ME

Message: *Live as an ambassador for Christ.* Read the following Scriptures and meditate on these truths for a while. Let them simmer in your spirit before moving on.

Acts 9:3–4: "As he neared Damascus on his journey, suddenly a light from heaven flashed around him. He fell to the ground and heard a voice say to him, 'Saul, Saul, why do you persecute me?'"

Acts 9:17: "Then Ananias went to the house and entered it. Placing his hands on Saul, he said, 'Brother Saul, the Lord—Jesus, who appeared to you on the road as you were coming here—has sent me so that you may see again and be filled with the Holy Spirit.'

2 Corinthians 5:17: "Therefore, if anyone is in Christ, the new creation has come: The old has gone, the new is here!"

Missional: Take a few moments and reflect on your life. Are you living like Saul or like Paul? How can you use your time, treasures, and talents to serve others in your circles of influence? Pray and ask God to show you areas in your life you can give back for the kingdom of God.

Meditate: I pray you are trusting and walking in the purpose God has destined for your life—a unique purpose that uses your time, treasures, and talents for the kingdom of God.

Heavenly Father,

Thank You for giving me gifts that I can use to advance the kingdom of God to those around me. Help me continue to serve others well with a thankful and generous heart. You are my Rock and Redeemer.

In Jesus's name, Amen

SERVING OTHERS: A PATH TO PEACE

I want to encourage you today: stop and pray. Ask the Lord, *Who can I help today?* Take the focus off yourself and bless another person through your actions and your words. The Lord is in the blessing.

Do you wake up feeling like you have nothing more to give? Are you tired and drained from life's daily grind, wondering to yourself, *What is this all for?* Are you looking for relief and peace that never seems to come? Are you burning the candle at both ends, lacking the fire to keep the flame burning? What causes us to continue living in constant busyness, creating a space that leaves us riddled with anxiousness and exhaustion? How can we help others if we are overbooked in our lives? Do you say yes to everything and everyone? This might be hard to hear and do, but stop living for a future that is not promised. Love like today was your last, and live like you are driven by something more than yourself. Love like Jesus. Live for the kingdom of God. There is purpose in His promises.

John 15:12 tells us, "My command is this: Love each other as I have loved you." This means loving those around you well. This may mean sacrificing your comfort or time for another, giving of yourself freely without wanting something in return, just being there for another. This requires you to reflect and evaluate what you deem important in your life. What areas can you give up to create spaces to serve others? Are you using your time, treasures, and talents to expand the kingdom of God? Do you use your free time wisely?

You need spaces in your day to spend time with God, resting in His promises. You also need areas in your life that bring you fulfillment and peace, like hobbies and spending quality time with family and friends. But oftentimes, many of us fill our time with activities that exhaust us, or we put too much on our agenda. We begin to lack time for God, which tends to leave us drained and depleted. What areas of your life can you let go of to make time for God and others? How can you create spaces that allow you to rest, giving you energy to serve and love others well?

I have had to learn through discipline to take time to spend with the Lord. The time I spent doing things that were mind-numbing or that I thought brought me peace pales in comparison to my intimate time with the Lord. I have gained clarity, wisdom, and peace. My daily devotion takes the focus off me and puts it on my reverence for the Lord, which allows me to walk in Spirit and truth in my daily life. I am more likely to help and see the world around me through God's eyes rather than my own. I find that blessing others impacts me more than the person I am helping. I try to see people the way God does. Looking through the lens of love allows me to have a deeper and more compassionate attitude toward others, giving me the capacity and endurance to keep serving the world around me well.

MAKING IT ABOUT ME

Message: *Serve others with a generous heart.* Read the following Scripture and meditate on this truth for a while. Let it simmer in your spirit before moving on.

> John 15:12: "My command is this: Love each other as I have loved you."

Missional: Take a few moments and reflect on how you can love generously. How can spending time with the Lord daily change how you see and help others? What are some ways you can serve another today?

Meditate: I pray you find time to rest in the Lord and focus your time, energy, and gifts on a greater purpose. Be a blessing to someone today.

Heavenly Father,

Thank You for Your goodness and Your faithfulness over my life. Help me continue to love others well by giving my time and resources to help spread Your love to the world around me, giving You all the glory.

In Jesus's name, Amen

GRATITUDE: MEDICINE FOR THE SOUL AND FUEL FOR SERVICE

I want to encourage you today to spend time with the Lord, thanking Him for all your blessings. Gratitude is medicine for the soul. Thankfulness leads to a serving heart for those around you. Live today with gratitude and a helpful heart.

Do you wake up already defeated before the day begins? Do you struggle with anxious thoughts? Do your thoughts or doubts leave you feeling helpless or depressed? Do your negative thoughts tend to take control of you, rendering you paralyzed with fear or doubt? Do you have a hard time finding a positive outlook based on your circumstances? Are you living in a cycle of doom and gloom, not recognizing the goodness in your life and allowing your circumstances to dictate your happiness and peace? Are you letting your flesh take control of what you know to be true in your spirit? A state of constant fear and anxiety will leave you paralyzed and stagnant in life. You will not grow into who God called you to be. Your thoughts and feelings need to align with truth in order to recognize God's promises rather than your own feelings or the lies of the enemy. I often struggle with these same questions as I combat the vicious cycle of emotional roller coasters in my own life. It is not easy when you face hard circumstances to have a positive outlook. It takes discipline to train your mind to take the focus off yourself and approach it with gratitude.

A good way to combat the pattern of negative emotions is to take a moment every morning to take the focus off yourself and put it on those around you. Pray and allow the Holy Spirit to guide you into all truth. Wake up every morning with a different perspective. Think of how you can be a blessing to someone else rather than yourself. You are meant to serve others and spread the love of Jesus in all you do. Your calling is tied to your faith. Faith is your act of obedience that leads you to walk into God's will for your life. A heart that is focused on gratitude and thanksgiving has no space for anxiety or negative thoughts or patterns. You will live life with purpose and humility, serving the world around you well.

Matthew 20:28 tells us, "Just as the Son of Man did not come to be served, but to serve, and to give his life as a ransom for many." This verse emphasizes that true greatness in God's kingdom is found in serving others, not in seeking to be served. Our role here on earth is to emulate the life of Jesus as a servant leader, demonstrating humility and selflessness in all that we do.

A serving heart is a heart full of meaning and purpose, leading you to fulfill your kingdom destiny. Colossians 3:23–24 says, "Whatever you do, work at it with all your heart, as working for the Lord, not for human masters, since you know that you will receive an inheritance from the Lord as a reward. It is the Lord Christ you are serving."

Everything we do as Christians is for the Lord. Our attitude should be one of enthusiasm, dedication, and wholehearted effort, as if we are serving Jesus Himself. How do you serve Jesus? Do you do it begrudgingly, or with an attitude of gratitude? Everything we do should be to the glory of God.

One of my favorite Scriptures I pray over myself when faced with overwhelming emotions is 2 Timothy 1:7: "For the Spirit God gave us does not make us timid, but gives us power, love and self-discipline." This passage encourages believers to trust in the Holy Spirit's power, love, and self-control, rather than giving in to fear and doubt. It emphasizes that the Spirit transforms believers, empowering them to live courageous and impactful lives for God.

I recently was in a car collision with my daughter. I am thankful we both only had minor injuries. The driver of the other vehicle was at fault. Even though I knew there was nothing I could have done to avoid the collision, it still had me questioning my actions leading up to the crash. I was replaying it over and over in my mind.

The day had started out so beautifully. I went for my daily prayer run and was taking my daughter to church to serve in Vacation Bible School for the day. I remember thanking the Lord that morning and rejoicing about how far I had come since my concussion six months prior. Then out of nowhere, Boom! My day took a turn. Never did I question the goodness of God, but I did struggle to understand how this could have happened. I was playing the blame game with myself. This is my flesh that tries to defeat and take hold of my spirit. In the midst of the accident, there were many blessings. We both were calm and had peace that surpasses all understanding in the middle of the chaos: a Good Samaritan stopping to pray for us, a friend coming to help and pray, friends and family checking in on us, and a husband taking control of things so we could rest and relax. That to me is blessing beyond measure. I was witnessing others serving me with thankful and grateful hearts. I am learning to let go of the things that are out of my control. Fear can set in and leave me anxious and stop me from living the life God has called me to live. I have had to pray God's promises over me since the collision. I wake up grateful and thankful for all the beautiful blessings in my life. I have to choose JOY over fear every day. I have walked in some hard spaces, and this can easily try to defeat my progress if I let it. I am living my life with gratitude, serving others with a thankful heart. The Lord is my strength and stronghold.

MAKING IT ABOUT ME

Message: *Do everything in faith and to the glory of God.* Read the following Scriptures and meditate on these truths for a while. Let them simmer in your spirit before moving on.

Matthew 20:28: "Just as the Son of Man did not come to be served, but to serve, and to give his life as a ransom for many."

Colossians 3:23–24: "Whatever you do, work at it with all your heart, as working for the Lord, not for human masters, since you know that you will receive an inheritance from the Lord as a reward. It is the Lord Christ you are serving."

2 Timothy 1:7: "For the Spirit God gave us does not make us timid, but gives us power, love and self-discipline."

Missional: Take a few moments and reflect on how you can serve and love like Jesus with your family, friends, and community. Take time to write down areas of your life that hold you back from sharing your time and resources and helping others. How can you take time out of your day or week to give back to your community?

Meditate: I pray you choose JOY as you serve others with a heart full of gratitude for the Lord.

Heavenly Father,

Thank You for not giving me a spirit of fear, but of love, power, and a sound mind. Help me love others well and draw them closer to You through my actions and my words. You are my strong tower and fortress in every season.

In Jesus's name, Amen

THE UNSEEN HAND: GOD'S REFINING LOVE

I want to encourage you to draw strength from the well of hope and press into your faith, which is being refined and purified, to live on mission for the kingdom of God.

Are you feeling weak and drained from the world and all its troubles? Do you let your mind dwell too long in places that leave you discouraged, empty, or unsatisfied? Do you find yourself in hard circumstances that seem too difficult to handle in your own strength? Do you ever wonder why, when we are living life and striving to do good, bad things happen to us and we are faced with trials and difficult circumstances that seem to come out of nowhere? And they just seem to keep coming and we feel like throwing in the towel, begging for some relief from the constant storms of life? This, my friend, is part of our battle on this side of heaven, but take heart—Jesus overcame the world and is fighting our battles and is with us through them. We must draw near to the Lord and dwell in His promises, rejoicing always. There is power and purpose in our pain.

Isaiah 48:10 (ESV) tells us, "Behold, I have refined you, but not as silver; I have tried you in the furnace of affliction." This verse highlights how God purifies and strengthens His people through trials. Our struggles draw us closer to God and make us more like Him. This verse implies that God allows struggles in our lives to refine us in a way that allows us to grow and learn to be more like Jesus.

First Peter 1:7 says, "These have come so that the proven genuineness of your faith—of greater worth than gold, which perishes even though refined by fire—may result in praise, glory and honor when Jesus Christ is revealed." Believers are encouraged to see challenges as chances to strengthen their faith and draw closer to God. This view suggests that enduring difficulties now will lead to a more significant reward when Christ comes back. Hold fast to the profession of your faith. Stand firm and trust the Lord in the midst of your struggles. You have an opportunity to grow and bless those around you as you endure hardships, giving God all the glory. You are being purified and refined for something greater.

We have an opportunity to live out our faith every day. Faith is an action of obedience and belief, the assurance of things hoped for, the conviction of things not seen. As Christians, our faith object is Jesus. We are called to love God and love one another as Jesus first loved us. It is a privilege to participate in the lives of others, bringing life, light, and freedom to unredeemed spaces. Trials will come, but we must view them differently. We must view them as opportunities to grow in Christ, allowing the Holy Spirit to strengthen us through the trial and sharing our struggles with the people around us, allowing ourselves to be humble and vulnerable to encourage and deepen their faith. Hebrews 10:24–25 (ESV) tells us, "And let us consider how to stir up one another to love and good works, not neglecting to meet together, as is the habit of some, but encouraging one another, and all the more as you see the Day drawing near." This verse cries out to Christians to be intentional and gather regularly, fostering spiritual growth among believers. As believers, we should encourage ourselves proactively and consider how to inspire and support one another, displaying our faith through acts of love and good deeds.

There is purpose and healing through our pain. We must draw near to God and trust His plans for us, allowing the Holy Spirit to do His work in and through us. Spending time in prayer regularly, reading your Bible daily, and gathering in some form of biblical community, stirring each other up toward love and good deeds, are essential to living out your faith and living with a kingdom mindset. You are not meant to do this life alone. We need each other.

I am on a journey of faith just like you. I have had my share of good days and bad days. I struggle with sin just like you, and I have had cyclical patterns of sin in my life. I have walked through many trials and hard circumstances that felt unbearable. I can testify and have witnessed the power in the name of Jesus. I have studied the Bible, read many Christian self-help books, and listened to countless sermons from many pastors during almost two decades of following Jesus. I have a desire and a passion for knowing and emulating the life of Jesus and sharing it with you. I remember a time, even as a believer, when I didn't feel worthy to walk into a church because I didn't read the Bible. I felt judged by anyone who would talk about religion. I thought I needed to be a better version of what God wanted me to be to enter His sanctuary. I felt ashamed and guilty and completely condemned. But the Lord never stopped pursuing me through many vessels of hope.

I recall one particular seed planted in my life that really changed my heart. I overheard friends at my son's fifth birthday party chatting about a Bible study they were attending. I thought to myself, *I would never be capable of doing that in my life*. I was so far off from being that Proverbs 31 woman. But God was stirring my heart way back then. I began searching for a church. I'd prayed all my life to know Jesus. God led me three times to a particular church that I still attend today—a church that goes through the Bible line by line, teaching, giving historical background from the beginning to the end, centered on Jesus. The Lord's provisions and providence in my life are remarkable. I now serve the world around me, spreading the love of Jesus wherever I go through my actions and my words. I have had the privilege to lead women's Bible studies, help women through biblical lay counseling, serve in kids' ministry, and be part of the prayer team at my church. There is power in the name of Jesus. You are called to live a life on mission with a kingdom mindset, leading to your calling and God-given purposes. Do not believe the lies of the enemy. You are worthy. You are chosen. You are His.

This past Sunday I was sitting in church listening to the sermon on the book of Hebrews. A verse jumped off the page and into my heart. It was like the Holy Spirit illuminated this passage. It is exactly how I feel and how I want to live out the rest of my earthly life. Hebrews 13:15–16 says, "Through Jesus, therefore, let us continually offer to God a sacrifice of praise—the fruit of lips that openly profess his name. And do not forget to do good and to share with others, for with such sacrifices God is pleased."

The passage encourages a life of worship that isn't just about what we say but also about how we act. It highlights that our practical acts of service and generosity, offered through Christ, are just as important as our verbal praise. Ultimately, God is pleased when believers not only worship Him with their words but also demonstrate love and compassion by sharing what they have with others. This is my mission in life, and I pray it's your mission in life as well.

MAKING IT ABOUT ME

Message: *God's refining power is at work in your life.* Read the following Scriptures and meditate on these truths for a while. Let them simmer in your spirit before moving on.

> Isaiah 48:10 (ESV): "Behold, I have refined you, but not as silver; I have tried you in the furnace of affliction."

> 1 Peter 1:7: "These have come so that the proven genuineness of your faith—of greater worth than gold, which perishes even though refined by fire—may result in praise, glory and honor when Jesus Christ is revealed."

> Hebrews 13:15–16: "Through Jesus, therefore, let us continually offer to God a sacrifice of praise—the fruit of lips that openly profess his name. And do not forget to do good and to share with others, for with such sacrifices God is pleased."

Missional: Take a few moments and reflect on how God has redeemed areas in your life and how you can share with others the goodness of God. What are some practical ways you can serve others that enhance the kingdom of God? What are three things God has restored in your life? Take a moment to thank God.

Meditate: I pray you draw near to the Lord, submitting to Him in all your ways, trusting He has a plan and a purpose for you that is meant to be shared. You are His, and He is yours. Love like Jesus today.

Heavenly Father,

Thank You for restoring and redeeming me from the pits of my despair. Help me to serve others in loving and sharing Your faithfulness to me. You are my refuge and redeemer.

In Jesus's name, Amen

NEVER STOP PRAYING: YOUR HARVEST AWAITS

I want to encourage you to never stop praying and knocking on heaven's door. The Lord hears every word. He will answer in His timing and in His will for your good and His glory.

Are you weary and waiting on God to come and rescue you from your pain and suffering, or are you in a season that is overflowing with milk and honey? Have you thanked God and given Him praise today for the season you are in? Each season has a purpose and is leading us closer to our kingdom destiny. Droughts in our lives equip and prepare us for what is ahead. We typically do not see or have a clear vision of what's coming; we must trust God and His provision. He knows when the rain is coming and when the drought will end. He knows that the land will produce a harvest that bears much fruit. Keep your eyes on Jesus and keep praising and praying.

You are being prepared for greater things. God's providence and provision are perfect and unique in each person's life. Unlocking your potential is living a life of obedience to God's will; it is a constant act of faith and surrender of self. As Hosea 10:12 tells us: "Sow righteousness for yourselves, reap the fruit of unfailing love, and break up your unplowed ground; for it is time to seek the LORD, until he comes and showers his righteousness on you." This verse emphasizes repentance and spiritual renewal—a call to cultivate a life of obedience that is pleasing to God through our actions and our words. It is time to seek the Lord and walk in obedience so that He may come and rain His righteousness upon you.

Matthew 3:8 says, "Produce fruit in keeping with repentance." This verse means that true repentance is turning away from sin, not just acknowledging it. You must actively change your behavior to align with God's will through obedience.

Mark 4:26–29 says: "He also said, 'This is what the kingdom of God is like. A man scatters seed on the ground. Night and day, whether he sleeps or gets up, the seed sprouts and grows, though he does not know how. All by itself the soil produces grain—first the stalk, then the head, then the full kernel in the head. As soon as the grain is ripe, he puts the sickle to it, because the harvest has come.'" This parable reminds believers to faithfully sow the Word of God, trust in God's timing and power for growth, and be patient, knowing that God will work it out in His perfect timing and season in our lives.

There is power in prayer and living a life in obedience to God. Your heart and will are being transformed daily to be more like Jesus. Cling to that promise. Never give up the hope we have in Jesus. Keep praying, seeking, and knocking on heaven's door. I have witnessed God move in my life in ways that I know could only be Him. I continue to seek and pray God's will over my life and the lives around me. There is power in prayer, and it works! All prayers will be answered in His timing. Praise and worship the Lord in the season of waiting.

Psalm 126:5–6 has brought me through some tough seasons. It teaches me to never give up when pain comes, because joy is behind it. It says, "Those who sow with tears will reap with songs of joy. Those who go out weeping, carrying seed to sow, will return with songs of joy, carrying sheaves with them." Perseverance through hard trials will lead to a joyful reward. Never give up, and keep moving forward one day at a time. Don't stop praying!

MAKING IT ABOUT ME

Message: *Don't stop praying.* Read the following Scriptures and meditate on these truths for a while. Let them simmer in your spirit before moving on.

> Hosea 10:12: "Sow righteousness for yourselves, reap the fruit of unfailing love, and break up your unplowed ground; for it is time to seek the LORD, until he comes and showers his righteousness on you."

> Matthew 3:8: "Produce fruit in keeping with repentance."

> Mark 4:26–29: "He also said, 'This is what the kingdom of God is like. A man scatters seed on the ground. Night and day, whether he sleeps or gets up, the seed sprouts and grows, though he does not know how. All by itself the soil produces grain—first the stalk, then the head, then the full kernel in the head. As soon as the grain is ripe, he puts the sickle to it, because the harvest has come.'"

> Psalm 126:5–6: "Those who sow with tears will reap with songs of joy. Those who go out weeping, carrying seed to sow, will return with songs of joy, carrying sheaves with them."

Missional: Take a few moments and reflect on how you have been sowing seeds in your life. How can you plant seeds of hope in the lives around you by sharing the gospel? Write down how God has harvested some of the seeds you have sown in your life.

Meditate: I pray you never give up and walk in faith each day, knowing you are a fighter and one day you will reap a harvest.

Heavenly Father,

Thank You for giving me the strength to sow in tears and continue fighting my battles in Your mighty power. Help me grow in my faith and share with the world around me the goodness and mercy of Your loving hand on my life.

In Jesus's name, Amen

WHEN GOD SINGS OVER YOU: DISCOVERING HIS JOY AND UNFAILING LOVE

I want to encourage you today to stop and rest with the Lord. He takes great delight in you. Put your hope in His unfailing love.

Do you ever feel like you are always busy, with no more to give? Is your energy depleted by the time you hit the pillow at night? Do you spend every moment striving to be better than you were yesterday, for yourself and those around you? Have you ever wondered if they even notice, or if you do all these wonderful deeds in vain? Are you someone that lets the day go by, and before you know it, it's evening and you forgot to spend time with the Lord? Then you have to battle the guilt monster that keeps feeding you lies, telling you that you are not being a good Christian if you are not praying enough, reading your Bible enough, giving enough, serving enough—and the list can go on. You may feel like God is disappointed in you and you are not enough. This is where I have been at different seasons of my life.

I remember when the Holy Spirit illuminated a Scripture through a picture I stumbled upon, and I realized in that moment that I was enough and that Jesus delights in all of me, even when I feel I am not enough.

Zephaniah 3:17 says, "The Lord your God is with you, the Mighty Warrior who saves. He will take great delight in you; in his love he will no longer rebuke you, but will rejoice over you with singing."

This verse illustrates God's mighty presence in our lives. It shows His power and joy over His children. The Lord is our mighty savior who delights in us with gladness, bringing us peace through His love, and He rejoices over us with singing. This highlights God's active role in our lives as believers, providing both salvation and profound joy and peace.

Do you wonder why the Lord delights in us and why His unfailing love endures? Psalm 147:11 tells us: "The LORD delights in those who fear him, who put their hope in his unfailing love."

This verse sheds light on the importance of a relationship with God that is characterized by reverence and trust in Him. God delights in a humble heart that has a reverent fear of Him and has hope in His mercy, more than any other external quality. Psalm 37:4 tells us, "Take delight in the LORD, and he will give you the desires of your heart."

This verse emphasizes finding joy and satisfaction in a relationship with the Lord. When we align our will with God's will, our desires naturally align with His desires for us. This is not a promise to fulfill our selfish desires, but rather a promise about aligning one's heart with God's will as one grows closer in relationship with Him.

The desires of my heart have not always been what God wanted for me. He allowed me to grow and learn through my fleshly desires and choices, which ultimately led me back to Him. It has been a transformative process that organically changed my desires to align with the Lord's. I now desire what God does. It tends to come more naturally and easily. I pray more, I serve more, I read my Bible more, I give more, and the list goes on. I no longer live for me. I live out of what God has done for me, and I naturally want to love better.

MAKING IT ABOUT ME

Message: *The Lord is singing over you with gladness.* Read the following Scriptures and meditate on these truths for a while. Let them simmer in your spirit before moving on.

Zephaniah 3:17: "The LORD your God is with you, the Mighty Warrior who saves. He will take great delight in you; in his love he will no longer rebuke you, but will rejoice over you with singing."

Psalm 147:11: "The LORD delights in those who fear him, who put their hope in his unfailing love."

Psalm 37:4: "Take delight in the LORD, and he will give you the desires of your heart."

Missional: Take a few moments and reflect on God's unfailing love for you. How has the Lord brought you out of darkness or tough circumstances? Write down ways you can seek the Lord in all you do. How can your desires change to be more like His?

Meditate: I pray you draw near to the Lord because He delights in you. He sings over you with gladness.

Heavenly Father,

Thank You for saving me and bringing me into Your kingdom of light. You sing over me with gladness. You are my mighty warrior.

In Jesus's name, Amen

PRAISE ANYWAY: A SONG OF PEACE

I want to encourage you to praise anyway. Let your adoration and devotion to the Lord carry you through your day.

Do you find it difficult to be positive when circumstances don't align with your will? Are you hyper-focused on the pain rather than the blessings amid the difficulties? Is there a silver lining or a rainbow in your cloudy day?

I know it can be very hard to have an optimistic view in everything we battle. But I can attest that if you draw near to the Lord and keep His praise on your lips, there is peace and calmness in every moment. This doesn't mean there's no struggle or a lack of pain, but it does ease it and keep you fighting and moving forward. There is power in our praise.

Psalm 150 tells us:

Praise the LORD. Praise God in his sanctuary; praise him in his mighty heavens. Praise him for his acts of power; praise him for his surpassing greatness. Praise him with the sounding of the trumpet, praise him with the harp and lyre, praise him with timbrel and dancing, praise him with the strings and pipe, praise him with the clash of cymbals, praise him with resounding cymbals. Let everything that has breath praise the LORD. Praise the LORD.

This is a powerful reminder that praise should be a central focus of our lives.

Ephesians 5:19 tells us, "Speaking to one another with psalms, hymns, and songs from the Spirit. Sing and make music from your heart to the Lord." This verse encourages believers to express their joy and thankfulness to the Lord. This is a result of being filled with the Holy Spirit, which will lead to heartfelt worship—singing praises, expressing gratitude, and building up one another in faith.

There is beauty in our pain. We may not see it right away, but in time, blessings will be revealed. I am reminded of a season of deep sorrow, a grief that had me tied up in knots. Losing my parents in my twenties shattered me to the core. I felt empty and very alone, even in a crowded room. My faith was shaken, and it led me to have anger and bitterness toward God.

My pain and bitterness led me down dark paths that brought me to my "Egypt." I was slowly running away from God without realizing it. I just stopped praying and started seeking to gratify my own desires to numb the hurt. Deep down, in the crevices of my soul, I knew God was there, and on occasion I would cry out, but this was only during those deep, dark nights. It took many years and many nudges from vessels of hope around me to ultimately lead me back to the loving arms of Jesus. My chains were broken, and I was set free from the bondage of my sin. I was redeemed and rescued from a life that could have had lasting consequences and changed my trajectory and God-given purposes. I am thankful Jesus pursued me in my darkest moments and led me out of my Egypt to His promised land. Praise and all the glory to God!

MAKING IT ABOUT ME

Message: *Praise anyway.* Read the following Scriptures and meditate on these truths for a while. Let them simmer in your spirit before moving on.

> Psalm 150: "Praise the LORD. Praise God in his sanctuary; praise
> him in his mighty heavens. Praise him for his acts of power; praise
> him for his surpassing greatness. Praise him with the sounding of
> the trumpet, praise him with the harp and lyre, praise him with
> timbrel and dancing, praise him with the strings and pipe, praise
> him with the clash of cymbals, praise him with resounding cymbals.
> Let everything that has breath praise the LORD. Praise the LORD."

Ephesians 5:19: "Speaking to one another with psalms, hymns, and songs from the Spirit. Sing and make music from your heart to the Lord."

Missional: Take a few moments and reflect on how you can praise today in the midst of your storm or circumstance. How has God brought you out of your "Egypt" into His promised land?

Meditate: I pray you find peace and stillness in the midst of every circumstance. May you worship the Lord, singing a loud, joyful noise of praise.

Heavenly Father,

Thank You for loving me and pursuing me even when praises were not on my lips. Help me see the good in everything. Keep my eyes on You. You are my song.

In Jesus's name, Amen

ACTION

ACTION—LIVING OUT THE PROMISES OF GOD AND
TRUSTING JESUS AS YOU PARTICIPATE IN HIS STORY.

*I have been crucified with Christ and I no longer live, but Christ
lives in me. The life I now live in the body, I live by faith in
the Son of God, who loved me and gave himself for me.*

GALATIANS 2:20

Action is pursuing the kingdom of God in everything you do. Living with a kingdom mindset keeps you focused on things above, bringing heaven here on earth. You have the privilege to work with God—participating in the lives of others, bringing redemption in dark spaces, and giving all the glory to God. God does not call us when we are ready or prepared. He equips us as we step out in faith. Martin Luther said, "God does not look for what he loves, he creates it." This means that God's love is not based on our inherent goodness or worthiness; rather, it is God's love that makes us worthy of love. We are His workmanship, like a potter creating something beautiful with his clay. God's love is creative, not like human love, which is reactive, based on our qualities that are lovely. God makes the unlovable lovable. Living in action for the kingdom of God leads us to our divine purpose. We live out the promises of God, allowing the Holy Spirit to transform our lives as we live on mission for the kingdom of God.

THE POWER OF YOUR PAIN

I want to continue to encourage you to cling to your faith and share the hope you have in Jesus with those around you. It may cost you everything, but there is power in your testimony.

Are you struggling or walking in circumstances that feel overwhelming? Are you living in your pain and hardship alone in silence? Are you afraid to share your struggle with another person for fear of what they will think? Or maybe you are struggling and want to share but don't know where to start. Let me tell you that there is power in your pain.

Second Timothy 1:7–8 (ESV) tells us, "For God gave us a spirit not of fear but of power and love and self-control. Therefore, do not be ashamed of the testimony about our Lord, nor of me his prisoner, but share in suffering for the gospel by the power of God." This passage clearly teaches us that God did not give us a spirit of fear. Fear is not from God. Fear is a liar and must be cast out of our minds if we want to move in faith. Our strength is not of this world; it is a spiritual strength and an ability to endure suffering and speak God's Word with boldness. This is powerful and can be beneficial to others as we persevere and endure suffering through sharing our faith. The spirit of love signifies a selfless, righteous love that motivates acts of self-surrender for the benefit of those around us. Therefore, the apostle Paul goes on to tell us that suffering for the gospel is a part of the Christian life, and believers should be willing to share in that suffering with others persecuted for their faith. We can endure and persevere in our suffering with courage and confidence through the power of God.

We live in a changing culture—a worldly culture that seems to cancel anything that does not align with its agenda. It can be disheartening and leave us feeling anxious and oftentimes frustrated. We may feel like we are outcasts in a hell-bent world, but take heart—you are not of this world. How do we navigate this world as believers without becoming absorbed or entangled in the culture around us? It can be easy to lose our self-control in a world that screams at us to live for ourselves and the comforts this world has to offer. Do you find yourself bending to the culture or to your beliefs?

I find it takes a constant remembering of what Christ has done for me to keep my eyes on things above and the kingdom purposes God has for me while I am here. Suffering is part of that process. I have learned to praise in the suffering and share in that suffering, encouraging others to live with a kingdom mindset. I, like you, will always have rivals in my inner and outer circles of influence. These people are far from God or do not understand the depths and heights of the gospel. I choose to be bold in my faith to share the good news because I know something that will have eternal consequences for the person I am encouraging. It may cost me everything when I stand with Jesus rather than cultural norms or those that are anti-Jesus or false doctrines and theology. They do not know the truth. John 8:32 says, "Then you will know the truth, and the truth will set you free." Many are in bondage to sin and do not even know it. The culture tells them it's okay or that "God is love."

There are many "gods" that tickle the ears but do not convict the heart, leaving you in a cycle of sin with no true repentance. Jesus is the way, the truth, and the life. He is the way to the Father. He died for you so you would have forgiveness of sin, a debt you cannot pay on your own. Putting your trust in Jesus and believing God raised Him to life is your salvation from this life to eternity with Him. Nothing you do can bring this saving grace, only your faith. Jesus suffered for us, and He calls us to suffer for Him through our testimony of how the gospel saved us. We are no longer slaves or prisoners to our sin. We are clothed in His righteousness once we are saved.

Sharing in our suffering through engaging in the "prisonship of righteousness" brings freedom and a resurrected life. Stand up and proclaim your faith! You were once a slave to sin. Now, in Christ Jesus, you are a slave to righteousness—freedom.

MAKING IT ABOUT ME

Message: *Praise through the pain—the Lord has a purpose in our pain.* Read the following Scriptures and meditate on these truths for a while. Let them simmer in your spirit before moving on.

> 2 Timothy 1:7–8 (ESV): "For God gave us a spirit not of fear but of power and love and self-control. Therefore, do not be ashamed of the testimony about our Lord, nor of me his prisoner, but share in suffering for the gospel by the power of God."

> John 8:32: "Then you will know the truth, and the truth will set you free."

Missional: Take a few moments and reflect on your life and how your struggles and trials have shaped who you are in Christ today. How have you seen God's unseen hand working in your life? Write down the areas of your life where you can serve others and help, areas that you have struggled in or may be struggling in now.

Meditate: I pray, even if it's difficult, that you keep pushing toward the pursuit of righteousness through the gospel of Jesus Christ. Endure in the suffering and praise through the pain. The Lord will redirect your suffering for your good and His glory! The power of the gospel is in your suffering and your testimony.

Heavenly Father,

Thank You for my struggles because I know that You are working them out for my good and for Your good purposes. Help me and strengthen me so I can be a vessel of hope and love to those around me and those that may need encouragement. You are my help in times of trouble. I praise You through every trial and will give You all the glory!

In Jesus's powerful name, Amen

THE GOOD THING: SUSTENANCE FOR A SERVING HEART

I want to encourage you today to find rest in Jesus. He is your good portion. Do you overbook yourself? Do you say yes and then later regret it when you realize you've added too much to your calendar each day? Do you tend to take on too much, with every good intention to keep everything afloat and see it to fruition? I tend to say yes, and keep saying yes with all the momentum and energy, until I realize that I just can't do it all, and I get overwhelmed or start getting sick because I am burning the candle at both ends. Serving the world around me without stopping and taking a breath to rest, to refresh, and to replenish my soul. I need to take time to do the good thing so I can continue doing good with a healthy and happy heart.

What is the good thing that sustains us and keeps us in a state of continued rest?

I am reminded of one of my favorite stories in the Bible, a story that continues to teach me: the story of Martha and Mary. These two sisters were friends of Jesus, and both had very good intentions one day when Jesus came with His disciples to visit their home in Bethany. Luke 10:38–40 says, "As Jesus and his disciples were on their way, he came to a village where a woman named Martha opened her home to him. She had a sister called Mary, who sat at the Lord's feet listening to what he said. But Martha was distracted by all the preparations that had to be made. She came to him and asked, 'Lord, don't you care that my sister has left me to do the work by myself? Tell her to help me!"

Martha had good intentions and a gift for serving, but she was missing the heart of discipleship. Martha was more concerned about the act of serving Jesus and His disciples and wanted help. She allowed herself to grow weary and frustrated, focusing on all her to-do lists and not her purpose, losing her ability to serve with a happy heart. Martha wanted to continue saying yes to her tasks, becoming hyper-focused on them and growing increasingly overwhelmed until she lost sight of the purpose for serving Jesus. Do you find yourself serving others with a frustrated heart like Martha? Let's look further at the passage. Verse 42 says, "But few things are needed—or indeed only one. Mary has chosen what is better, and it will not be taken away from her."

Jesus gently rebukes Martha for being anxious and worried about many things, and He praises Mary. Mary chose the good thing—being at the feet of Jesus and His teaching. This is the place of true rest, the place that leads to discipleship, the place we need to be in order to serve others well. At the feet of Jesus is the perfect place to rest, refuel, and recharge so we may serve others with grateful hearts.

I recently realized I was becoming more like Martha and needed to take time to sit at the feet of Jesus and be like Mary. I can sense when I start to get too busy, adding more than I can handle, even if the things I am doing are good things like ministry and community outreach. I am not going to serve and help others well if I am not sitting with Jesus, getting spiritual nourishment and living water daily. Being more like Mary prepared me to serve like Martha with a thankful heart.

If you are finding you do not have time or energy to spend time daily with Jesus, then it's time to take things off your plate. Rest in Him, and He will give you the spiritual energy and nourishment to live missionally for the kingdom of God.

MAKING IT ABOUT ME

Message: *Choose what is better, and it will not be taken from you.* Read the following Scriptures and meditate on these truths for a while. Let them simmer in your spirit before moving on.

> Luke 10:38–40: "As Jesus and his disciples were on their way, he came to a village where a woman named Martha opened her home to him. She had a sister called Mary, who sat at the Lord's feet listening to what he said. But Martha was distracted by all the preparations that had to be made. She came to him and asked, 'Lord, don't you care that my sister has left me to do the work by myself? Tell her to help me!'

> Luke 10:42: "But few things are needed—or indeed only one. Mary has chosen what is better, and it will not be taken away from her."

Missional: Take a few moments and reflect on how you have spent time at the feet of Jesus lately. What can you learn from God that can help you serve others well? What are ways you can be a good steward of your time today and sit with Jesus?

Meditate: I pray you find rest at the feet of Jesus today so you may live missionally, serving and loving others around you well.

Heavenly Father,

Thank You for loving me and allowing me to sit at Your feet and learn from Your teachings. Help me serve others well, using my time and treasures to enhance the kingdom of God.

In Jesus's name, Amen

LIVING FOR HIS KINGDOM: THE FRUIT OF A SURRENDERED LIFE

I want to encourage you today to give all your strengths and weaknesses to the Lord. Let go of your will and let the Holy Spirit work in and through you to surrender your demands and struggles to Him. Stop trying to control the outcome of your day. Walk in the Spirit and His will for you. Lift your eyes unto the hills where your help comes from and surrender your day to the Lord. You will find peace and purpose in His provisions for you.

Do you find yourself trying to figure out how you are going to get through your day before you even roll out of bed? Are you someone who needs to have a to-do list and struggles when you fall short and can't accomplish your goals in the manner you expected? Do your goals and desires align with the promises of God? Do you let your flesh determine your happiness?

Do you start the day with an agenda and its outcome and how you're going to accomplish it already in your mind? Is your success determined by the goal or the desired outcome of that goal? Do you let your will lead you in all circumstances, or do you let the Lord navigate and take the front seat in your life? Are you living for your kingdom or the kingdom of God? These questions are a good starting place to recognize and discern whether your heart has surrendered it all to Jesus, or if you are clinging to your own stubborn will, selfishness, and pride. How do we release our hopes, dreams, and aspirations to the Lord and let go of pursuing our own happiness? How do we surrender it all to the Lord no matter the outcome?

Galatians 5:24–25 says, "Those who belong to Christ Jesus have crucified the flesh with its passions and desires. Since we live by the Spirit, let us keep in step with the Spirit." Belonging to Christ means crucifying our former selves, and this passage calls us to live and act in alignment with the Holy Spirit. It emphasizes the importance of embodying the Spirit's fruit and actively avoiding behaviors that stand in opposition to it. Furthermore, it cautions against the destructive forces of pride, rebellion, and envy within the community of believers. God calls us to total surrender in life, urging us to walk in the Spirit so that our actions produce good works for His glory. Your desires must align with the promises of God to fully live out His will for your life. Fleshly desires put us out of alignment with the Holy Spirit and will lead us further from our purpose and the desires God has planned for us. Drawing near to God daily in prayer, worship, and reading His Word deepens our faith walk and changes our desires to His desires for us.

When we hold on to our will, we are living out of pride, not humility. Believers often ask the Lord to help them along their journey in life but tend to want the outcome to be their way and for their fleshly desires to be fulfilled. We often struggle to let the Lord into our mess and let Him clean it up His way. We want to control the process and the outcome. It is not an easy process to let go of our will, our selfishness, and our earthly desires. It is a living sacrifice. We must die to our flesh every day. We must give it all to the Lord daily and let His perfect will for us work in and through us.

Romans 12:1 says, "Therefore, I urge you, brothers and sisters, in view of God's mercy, to offer your bodies as a living sacrifice, holy and pleasing to God—this is your true and proper worship." This is a powerful call for believers to move beyond routine and religious practices and offer their entire being as a living sacrifice, a daily and active devotion to God's purpose. This act of worship leads you to a more fulfilling and desirable life.

Once you start living sacrificially and giving all your desires and will to Him, you will see transformation in your life. You will no longer live out of your own desires and selfish gain but the Lord's provision and perfect will for your life. Your natural tendency will be for your desires to align with God's desires for you. Romans 12:2 goes on to say, "Do not conform to the pattern of this world, but be transformed by the renewing of your mind. Then you will be able to test and approve what God's will is—his good, pleasing and perfect will." This verse emphasizes the importance of not letting worldly influences shape our thinking and behavior but instead allowing God to reshape our minds through His Word and truth, so we can discern His will for our lives. You will easily be influenced by the world around you if you do not have an intimate relationship with the Lord. You must know His Word to understand His will for you.

Absolute surrender requires our whole heart given as a living sacrifice, a heart of worship and humility with open hands to the Lord. Giving all of ourselves to Jesus—our time, treasures, and talents—to be used for the kingdom of God.

I read a book many years ago by Andrew Murray called *Absolute Surrender*. This book opened my eyes to the selfishness I had and helped me fully let go of my will and surrender it to Jesus. This quote by Andrew Murray is a beautiful testament to a surrendered life: "The highest glory of the creature is in being only a vessel, to receive and enjoy and show forth the glory of God. It can do this only as it is willing to be nothing in itself, that God may be all. Water always fills first the lowest places. The lower, the emptier a man lies before God, the speedier and the fuller will be the inflow of the divine glory."

I am reminded of one of my favorite verses in the Bible, John 15:5: "I am the vine; you are the branches. If you remain in me and I in you, you will bear much fruit; apart from me you can do nothing." This passage establishes Jesus as the vital source of life and spiritual nourishment for believers. The Father nurtures and maintains the vine, which is essential for its sustained growth and fruit in us. I remember meditating and praying Romans 12 many years ago at a pivotal moment on my faith journey, a time when I needed change and direction in my life. I asked the Holy Spirit to cleanse me of all my iniquities and that my desires would become God's desires. I wanted a more fruitful purpose in life, an abundant life lived on mission for Christ, a life that is pleasing and holy in His sight. This was a process of change and constant discipline in my daily rhythms and routines. The change was not instant but a refining-by-fire kind of process. There were many trials and tribulations that led me to lean in and draw near to the Lord and surrender my will. The Lord taught me to let go and allow Him to work everything out for my good and His glory. I am learning daily to let go of my desires, even if they are good, because they may not align with my kingdom purposes and God's will for me. I must pray daily and unceasingly; this is a beautiful relationship that requires communication both ways. I still make mistakes and let my flesh get the better of me some days, but I am convicted quickly, and I discern good and evil more easily. I am able to surrender it all to the Holy Spirit to work in and through me. His perfect and pleasing will has led me to a purpose-driven life for the kingdom of God.

MAKING IT ABOUT ME

Message: *A surrendered life bears much fruit.* Read the following Scriptures and meditate on these truths for a while. Let them simmer in your spirit before moving on.

> Galatians 5:24–25: "Those who belong to Christ Jesus have crucified the flesh with its passions and desires. Since we live by the Spirit, let us keep in step with the Spirit."

> Romans 12:1: "Therefore, I urge you, brothers and sisters, in view of God's mercy, to offer your bodies as a living sacrifice, holy and pleasing to God—this is your true and proper worship."

> John 15:5: "I am the vine; you are the branches. If you remain in me and I in you, you will bear much fruit; apart from me you can do nothing."

Missional: Take a few moments and allow the Holy Spirit to work in your heart to reveal areas you need to surrender to His will. Write them down and release these burdens to God.

Meditate: I pray that you let go of all your striving for something more and allow the Holy Spirit to work in and through you to bring you to a transformed life lived in Him. You have a kingdom purpose waiting to be discovered and brought to fruition. Surrender it all to Jesus!

Heavenly Father,

Thank You for being my True Vine. Help me remain in You as You remain in me. Teach me to abide. Your ways are higher and greater than mine.

In Jesus's name, Amen

TRUSTING GOD THROUGH THE WHIRLWIND: FINDING PEACE IN UNCERTAINTY

I want to encourage you to lean on the rock of your salvation. Keep your eyes off the storm and on the perfecter of your faith—Jesus. He is with you and will carry you through the storms of life. The Lord is your shepherd and your strength. Lean into His goodness and mercy today.

Are you struggling to understand why circumstances can change the rhythm and routines of our lives in an instant? Wondering why bad things happen to good people? In the blink of an eye, our whole life can turn upside down and even alter our trajectory. What we once thought was important and had our full attention and focus in our daily provisions can drastically change. As a matter of fact, the things we once stressed about no longer seem to matter. We can easily find ourselves stuck in a whirlwind of emotions, questioning how this can be happening. You may already know by now that storms are a part of life. How we walk through them is significant to how we sustain our peace and positive attitude through difficult trials. Do you find that you let your circumstances dictate your feelings? Do you allow your emotions to control and dictate your thought life? Are your feelings trumping your faith?

Proverbs 3:5 says, "Trust in the LORD with all your heart and lean not on your own understanding." This verse focuses on God's truth, wisdom, and guidance rather than our own feelings and personal understanding, even when they seem to contrast with God's. His ways are better and higher than ours.

We may not understand the pain and suffering, but there is a purpose and a plan that is being worked out for our good and God's glory. Blessings will come in and through a trial to strengthen and deepen our faith. Proverbs 3:6 (ESV) says, "In all your ways acknowledge him, and he will make straight your paths." This verse emphasizes the importance of acknowledging the Lord in our actions and decisions. We must seek direction and guidance from God, which ultimately will lead us to a clearer and more purposeful path. It can be difficult to let go and trust God with every part of us, especially when we are struggling and in pain. We tend to want to control the outcome, and understandably so. No one wants the trial to last too long.

I am learning, as I face trials, to respond in worship and praise. This tends to align my will with God's will and eases the suffering. I have made a conscious effort to pray and praise through the pain, which leads me to focus on God's purpose and provision in my life. When fear and doubt start to creep in, I remind myself of 2 Corinthians 10:5, which emphasizes that we should "take captive every thought to make it obedient to Christ," indicating that our thoughts and feelings should align with truth and our faith. If we let our emotions dictate our lives, it can hinder our relationship with God. We must have faith over fear, even in the midst of heightened emotion. Faith should override our feelings. Truth must take precedence over the toxicity in our minds. Doubt may scream at us to give up or try to diminish our efforts to keep fighting when it seems hopeless, but God is our refuge and our strength and controls the outcomes of our destiny and purpose. He is our hope and strong tower amid the peaks and valleys of life. He sustains us and holds it all together, even when we do not feel Him. He is working it all out for our good and His glory.

I recently walked through an unforeseen circumstance that left me a bit shaken. It was difficult because it could have ended differently. There was a moment while sitting in a hospital room that I realized that by the grace of God, I am still alive and breathing. I have one more day to be a blessing and to show God's grace to others. This was a hard one for me. It had me asking and pondering many questions that I really could not answer, but my mind went there anyway. Questions like, *Why did this happen? Could I have done something different that would have prevented this? Did this come from God? Why would God let this happen? Couldn't it have been avoided or maybe come with less pain and suffering? Will this ever get better? Will I go through this again?* All these questions I wrestled with for a while. But one day, I sat and prayed and asked God to help me through these doubts and fears. I asked God to let this trial be a blessing to others and bring glory to Him. I wanted to praise Him through the pain. I slowly started to gain my strength and courage back one day at a time. I no longer let the fear and my feelings determine my outcome. I will continue to do that today.

I may not know the "why," but I do know that it all works out for my good and God's glory. His ways are higher and better than mine.

MAKING IT ABOUT ME

Message: *Truth must take precedence over the toxicity in your mind.* Read the following Scriptures and meditate on these truths for a while. Let them simmer in your spirit before moving on.

> 2 Corinthians 10:5: "Take captive every thought to make it obedient to Christ."

> Proverbs 3:5: "Trust in the LORD with all your heart and lean not on your own understanding."

Missional: Take a few moments and let your faith determine the outcome of areas in your life that seem difficult or bring about fear and anxiety. Reflect on God's promises that will speak life into your circumstances.

Meditate: I pray you give all your worries and fears to God. He cares for you and will carry you through your pain. He has a purpose and a plan far bigger and greater than we could ever ask for or imagine. Rest in that truth today.

Heavenly Father,

Thank You for Your promises. They are good and speak life into my life. I take every thought captive to the obedience of Christ. I ask that You fill me with Your truth and wisdom and cast out any lies from the enemy. You are my deliverer.

In Jesus's mighty name, Amen

EMBRACE YOUR NEW BEGINNING: BE YOUR LIGHT

I want to encourage you to begin your day knowing it's going to be a new beginning, and be glad in it. Shine your light for all to see.

Do you start your day with all the things that need to get done, feeling defeated and exhausted before you even have your cup of coffee? Are you someone that puts expectations on your day, and if one thing goes wrong, then the whole day is ruined in your mind? Did you know that every day you have the potential to be the best at whatever you do? You have unique gifts and skills given to you by God to give and serve the world. You have the choice to make today a good day or not; you get to decide how you will react to every circumstance and encounter. As Psalm 118:24 (NKJV) says: "This is the day the LORD has made; We will rejoice and be glad in it."

This verse is a powerful pronouncement of faith and gratitude. It signifies that every day is a gift from God and a cause for rejoicing. You have to set your focus on the gifts of grace, which will cause your mind to shift its focus to gratitude and thankfulness. This changes how you will see the world around you. You must train your mind to shift its focus to a kingdom mindset.

Do you find yourself living every day for some future version of yourself? Do you live for tomorrow? Do you see today as an opportunity to achieve self-gain in areas of your life that only bring you glory? Are you living with your own kingdom agendas and goals?

Did you know that you were created for a far greater purpose than what the world beckons you to be or believe?

As Matthew 5:13 says: "You are the salt of the earth. But if the salt loses its saltiness, how can it be made salty again? It is no longer good for anything, except to be thrown out and trampled underfoot." This verse means believers are to be a positive and impactful force in the world, much like salt adds flavor and preserves food. However, if they abandon their faith and values, they become ineffective. The passage goes on to say (vv. 14–16), "You are the light of the world. A town built on a hill cannot be hidden. Neither do people light a lamp and put it under a bowl. Instead they put it on its stand, and it gives light to everyone in the house. In the same way, let your light shine before others, that they may see your good deeds and glorify your Father in heaven." This passage emphasizes that Christians should live lives that are visibly different and impactful, reflecting God's character and leading others to Him. We must shine our light every day, doing good to others and living lives that glorify God. You can be the salt and light to everyone in your circles and beyond. Imagine that calling and privilege you were given as a believer.

I find that if I focus my mind on things that are not kingdom-centered, I tend to live in fear, doubt, and defeat. I have to train my mind moment by moment to always have God's precepts that will shift my focus to my God-given purposes—to love God with all of my heart, mind, soul, and strength; make Him known with my actions and words; love others with grace; and serve the world with my time, treasures, and talents that were given to me by God.

MAKING IT ABOUT ME

Message: *Shift your focus to a kingdom mindset.* Read the following Scriptures and meditate on these truths for a while. Let them simmer in your spirit before moving on.

> Psalm 118:24 (NKJV): "This is the day the LORD has made; We will rejoice and be glad in it."

Matthew 5:13–16: "You are the salt of the earth. But if the salt loses its saltiness, how can it be made salty again? It is no longer good for anything, except to be thrown out and trampled underfoot. You are the light of the world. A town built on a hill cannot be hidden. Neither do people light a lamp and put it under a bowl. Instead they put it on its stand, and it gives light to everyone in the house. In the same way, let your light shine before others, that they may see your good deeds and glorify your Father in heaven."

Missional: Take a few moments and rejoice in the Lord and be glad, for He is the source of all things good. How can you shift your mindset to be more kingdom focused? What gifts has God given you that you can use to shed light into the world around you?

Meditate: I pray you walk in the light of God's glory and be salt and light to the world around you. Shift your mindset today.

Heavenly Father,

Thank You for this day and the beauty it holds. Help me be the light of grace to others and equip me to serve the world around me, giving You all the glory.

In Jesus's name, Amen

GOD'S MASTERPIECE: TRUSTING HIS PEN IN THE STORY OF YOUR LIFE

I want to encourage you to trust God in the details of your life. He is writing your story. I know it can be difficult to give up our control in every circumstance. We want everything to be perfect and to go our way. We want to be the author of our story. We want to have the power to know how our book ends. We want a fairy-tale or Hallmark version of our lives. This is not how God writes our story. If our lives had no struggles or pain, would we need rescue? Would we need a Savior in our story? When we face difficulties in life and those struggles are beyond our capacity to fix, we find ourselves in desperate need of a hero to rescue us from the pit of our despair.

We cry out and beg for redemption, and when it comes there is a sense of relief, bringing us peace and joy, drawing us to our Creator. This brings a deep sense of hope and assurance in our lives. We are not the author of our story. We are the paper, and God holds the pen. Jesus is the author and perfecter of our faith. He is the one who brings our story to depths and heights that help and shape our lives, leading us to our kingdom destiny. Are you ready to give God the pen and trust His writing process? Psalm 37:23 (NLT) says, "The LORD directs the steps of the godly. He delights in every detail of their lives." This verse emphasizes God's love for us in our everyday lives and suggests that He is in the details of our story.

One thing remains: God is the consistency in our lives. We may fail and get off track, but God directs our paths and makes the crooked road straight again. God never changes. Hebrews 13:8 tells us, "Jesus Christ is the same yesterday and today and forever." This verse emphasizes that the character and nature of Jesus never changes. This is a source of assurance, comfort, and peace to believers, knowing Jesus is reliable and faithful to us.

I am encouraged to know that I am not the author of my story. I see God in the details of my life. The Lord has edited and reworked pages and chapters of my story, adding and taking away characters, including plot twists, bringing conflict and tension, and deepening character development, with a consistent theme and redemptive message. I believe that Jesus knows how to write my story, and I give Him control to bring my book to fruition. Philippians 1:6 says, "Being confident of this, that he who began a good work in you will carry it on to completion until the day of Christ Jesus." This verse emphasizes God's commitment and faithfulness to His children. He will complete the process and transformation of spiritual growth in us. God's work is not a one-time event; it is an ongoing process that He will bring to completion.

MAKING IT ABOUT ME

Message: *God is in the details of your life.* Read the following Scriptures and meditate on these truths for a while. Let them simmer in your spirit before moving on.

> Psalm 37:23 (NLT): "The LORD directs the steps of the godly. He delights in every detail of their lives."

> Hebrews 13:8: "Jesus Christ is the same yesterday and today and forever."

> Philippians 1:6: "Being confident of this, that he who began a good work in you will carry it on to completion until the day of Christ Jesus."

Missional: Take a few moments and look over your life and see where God was in the details. Look how His unseen hand was editing parts of your story. What comes to mind? Write down the plot and redemptive parts of your story.

Meditate: I pray that you trust Jesus in the writing process of your life. He is author and finisher of your story. Give Him the pen and let go of control, knowing He writes with a purpose. He will bring you to your kingdom destiny.

Heavenly Father,

Thank You for being the author and sustainer of my story. Help me let go of the pen that I can grip so tightly at times in my life. I want to let go and trust You with all of me. You are author and finisher of my faith.

In Jesus's name, Amen

THE UNSTOPPABLE FLAME: THE POWER OF INTIMACY

I encourage you to grow in intimacy with the Lord. Spend time learning and practicing disciplines of faith. Allow the Holy Spirit to guide you into a deeper connection with Jesus.

Do you have faith larger than a mustard seed? Does your faith waver in difficult spaces and circumstances?

Does your faith change depending on the outcome of a situation, or does it remain constant? Do you spend time with God consistently, or only when you need Him? Did you know there are spiritual practices called *disciplines of the faith*? These practices strengthen our faith and transform our mindset. They will draw us nearer to and in deeper relationship with God. I read a book many years ago on the disciplines of the faith by Richard J. Foster called *Celebration of Discipline*. He wrote, "The purpose of Spiritual Disciplines is the total transformation of the person." Practicing spiritual disciplines will lead us into a deeper intimacy with the Lord, shifting our mindset to align with God's will. *There are many practices, such as worship, silence, meditation, simplicity, Scripture reading, fasting, prayer, and several more that deepen your connection with Jesus.*

First Chronicles 16:29 says, "Ascribe to the LORD the glory due his name; bring an offering and come before him. Worship the LORD in the splendor of his holiness." This Scripture encourages believers to give glory to God and worship him alone. Do you spend time worshiping God and thanking Him for all He's done for you?

There are many forms of worship, but I am always drawn to worshiping God through songs and hymns. I remember a time when Christian music was not my thing. I didn't understand this music or have a desire to listen to it on the radio. I thought it all sounded the same. It wasn't until I started attending church and I heard the songs through praise and worship that God opened my heart and ears to His music. I remember the first time I heard a song on our local Christian radio station and realized they sang it at the church I attended. It brought tears to my eyes, and to this day when I hear that song it brings me immense joy. Praise and worship is something I can do anywhere. Worship music is what God used to tickle my ears when I was far away from him.

Matthew 21:22 (KJV) says, "And all things, whatsoever ye shall ask in prayer, believing, ye shall receive." The Scripture emphasizes the power of faith and prayer. Matthew 17:20–21 tells us that Jesus said, "Because you have so little faith. Truly I tell you, if you have faith as small as a mustard seed, you can say to this mountain, 'Move from here to there,' and it will move. Nothing will be impossible for you." This passage illustrates the power of God that flows through the believer with even the smallest bit of faith. This is a good reminder that God can work miracles in our lives and we can participate in His work through faith. Prayer is another spiritual discipline that draws us closer to God. We can come to the throne of grace anytime and lay our burdens down at the feet of Jesus. We get to communicate with the creator and sustainer of all things and have a close relationship with Him. If you draw near to the Lord, He will draw near to you. There is power in prayer and power in the name of Jesus. Prayer opens the communication between you and God and creates an intimate relationship. If you do not spend time with the Lord, how would you know His character or His voice? Prayer should be an integral part of a believer's life.

James 4:8 tells us, "Come near to God and he will come near to you." This verse is a call to believers to actively seek a closer relationship with God. In return, God will draw near to us. There are many practices for spiritual growth that will deepen your relationship with Jesus. The more you spend time with the Lord practicing the disciplines of the faith, the more you will grow and be transformed, living a life with purpose, leading you to your kingdom destiny.

MAKING IT ABOUT ME

Message: *Intimacy with God deepens your relationship with Him.* Read the following Scriptures and meditate on these truths for a while. Let them simmer in your spirit before moving on.

> 1 Chronicles 16:29: "Ascribe to the LORD the glory due his name; bring an offering and come before him. Worship the LORD in the splendor of his holiness."

> Matthew 17:20–21: "Because you have so little faith. Truly I tell you, if you have faith as small as a mustard seed, you can say to this mountain, 'Move from here to there,' and it will move. Nothing will be impossible for you."

> James 4:8: "Come near to God and he will come near to you."

Missional: Take a few moments and sit in silence with the Lord and meditate on the three Scriptures in today's message. Write down what spoke to your heart.

Meditate: I pray you take time worshiping, praising, praying, and meditating on His Word. Draw near to God today, and He will draw near to you. Intimacy grows passion, and passion ignites an unstoppable flame that can't be burned out.

Heavenly Father,

Thank You for loving me and allowing me to draw near to the creator and sustainer of all things. I praise You with my lips and worship You with all my heart. I long for more intimacy with You. You are my goodness and faithfulness that never leaves me nor forsakes me.

In Jesus's name, Amen

AIM

AIM—LIVING A LIFE TRANSFORMED BY GOD, DRIVING
YOU TO LIVE OUT YOUR KINGDOM DESTINY.

*Many are the plans in a person's heart, but it
is the Lord's purpose that prevails.*

PROVERBS 19:21

You were created for a purpose. Your life is not by chance. You have unique gifts, talents, and treasures hidden by God until He reveals them to you in His perfect timing. The key to unlocking your potential is to live life in obedience and surrender, stepping out in faith, trusting God's purpose and will for your life. A. W. Tozer points us in the right direction when he said, "To the child of God, there is no such thing as accident. He travels an appointed way. Accidents may indeed appear to befall him and misfortune stalk his way; but these evils will be so in appearance only and will seem evils only because we cannot read the secret script of God's hidden providence and so cannot discover the ends at which He aims. The man of true faith may live in the absolute assurance that his steps are ordered by the Lord." God's unseen hand is working in and through us on our journey of faith. Jeremiah 29:11 tells us: "'For I know the plans I have for you,' declares the LORD, 'plans to prosper you and not to harm you, plans to give you hope and a future.'" This verse emphasizes that God is a driving force in shaping our lives and His desire is for our well-being. We are called to live on mission for the kingdom of God, bringing light, life, and freedom to the world around us. Our aim in life has a purpose and will lead us to our kingdom destiny.

A SPIRITUAL AWAKENING: FINDING LASTING FIRE FOR THE LORD

I want to encourage you today to keep going and continue loving and encouraging those around you. Never give up hope. Even in the darkest and driest spaces, the Lord is always working. His timing and will are perfect.

Do you have moments or even seasons when you just want to crawl into bed for days and shut the world out? Do you ever feel like you just want to stop doing the day-to-day, mundane, and repetitive tasks and demands of life that typically leave you overwhelmed or just plain burned-out? Maybe you find yourself going through the motions of life with no real sense of purpose, and you feel discouraged and defeated with no hope in sight.

Do you struggle to have lasting joy and peace even on your best days? I have been in those seasons and found that drawing near to God was the best remedy for my troubled heart. Jesus is better than anything this world has to offer.

I am reminded of a particular season of stress, fear, and anxiety that surrounded me. I went back to work after staying home with my kids for over seven years. I was entering a new field: teaching. Our family was not adjusting well to all the transitions. It was a busy time in our lives. I was going deeper in my walk with the Lord during this season and started seeing the world through a different lens. I started having a godly view and a contempt and scorn for things that once brought me worldly pleasure.

It was like my eyes were opened to the evil that easily tempted and enticed me. Everything seemed to be going wrong, and it kept getting worse. Family illnesses, job stress, and the heightened grief of losing my parents all seemed to converge in this season. I was in a perfect storm, a storm that led me to pray unceasingly one unforgettable night. The Lord drew near that night and gave me a tangible peace that surpassed all understanding, a gift that still carries me through the darkest night. The next morning, I opened my Bible and prayed. The Holy Spirit brought me to 1 Peter 1:3–7, which says:

Praise be to the God and Father of our Lord Jesus Christ! In his great mercy he has given us new birth into a living hope through the resurrection of Jesus Christ from the dead, and into an inheritance that can never perish, spoil or fade. This inheritance is kept in heaven for you, who through faith are shielded by God's power until the coming of the salvation that is ready to be revealed in the last time. In all this you greatly rejoice, though now for a little while you may have had to suffer grief in all kinds of trials. These have come so that the proven genuineness of your faith—of greater worth than gold, which perishes even though refined by fire—may result in praise, glory and honor when Jesus Christ is revealed.

This passage highlights God's grace, which bestows a dynamic hope on believers through Christ's rising from the dead, promising an eternal inheritance. It also emphasizes that enduring hardships is crucial for refining and authenticating our faith, ultimately leading to praise, glory, and honor at Jesus's return.

This was a defining moment on my journey of faith. It was a spiritual rebirth and awakening that stirred my spirit and gave me a lasting fire for the Lord that can never fade or burn out. My hope is no longer based on worldly things but on God's promises. Jesus is my living hope. Jesus is better than comfort, victory, sorrow, riches, or any worldly pleasure.

MAKING IT ABOUT ME

Message: *Jesus is our living hope.* Read the following Scripture and meditate on this truth for a while. Let it simmer in your spirit before moving on.

> 1 Peter 1:3–7: "Praise be to the God and Father of our Lord Jesus Christ! In his great mercy he has given us new birth into a living hope through the resurrection of Jesus Christ from the dead, and into an inheritance that can never perish, spoil or fade. This inheritance is kept in heaven for you, who through faith are shielded by God's power until the coming of the salvation that is ready to be revealed in the last time. In all this you greatly rejoice, though now for a little while you may have had to suffer grief in all kinds of trials. These have come so that the proven genuineness of your faith—of greater worth than gold, which perishes even though refined by fire—may result in praise, glory and honor when Jesus Christ is revealed."

Missional: Take a few moments and reflect on your living hope—Jesus. How has God been revealing Himself to you in your life? Write down all the things that come to mind when you think of Jesus. He is better than...?

Meditate: I pray your heart believes this truth today. You have an eternal hope in Jesus.

Heavenly Father,

Thank You for the hope I have in You. Help me endure the trials of this life with Your abiding presence. You are my living hope.

In Jesus's name, Amen

BREATHING LIFE: BECOMING GOD'S VOICE OF ENCOURAGEMENT

I want to encourage you to speak life into those around you. Uplift a family member, friend, coworker, or stranger today. Allow the Holy Spirit to infiltrate your every word. Season your conversations with grace and gentleness. Be the sunshine in someone's day.

Do you ever find yourself in conversations that make you uncomfortable or uneasy? Do you sit there and allow the conversation to continue if you know it is not uplifting? Are you someone who can walk away or even speak up against the flaming tongues, or do you stay quiet and listen? Do you allow the person who is not in the room, who is the center of conversation, to continue to be defamed? We all have been prone to these conversations and have let them linger. Most of us are not bold enough to stand against the majority, speaking life and extinguishing the flaming fire of the tongue. Ephesians 4:29 tells us: "Do not let any unwholesome talk come out of your mouths, but only what is helpful for building others up according to their needs, that it may benefit those who listen." This passage highlights the significance of speaking with grace and offering encouragement through our words. The verse suggests that those who are believers should choose kind, uplifting, and helpful conversations over language that wounds or discourages. Imagine if we only spoke to each other with wholesome talk and encouraged one another.

This would increase our sense of worth and love, rather than leaving us feeling defeated and discouraged. Do you want to be the person God called you to be by breathing life into another?

God calls us to live a life abundantly in Him, and every part of us should follow His commandments with our actions and words. The tongue has no bones, but it is the strongest part of our body because it can break the heart. There is power in your tongue.

James 3:9–12 tells us: "With the tongue we praise our Lord and Father, and with it we curse human beings, who have been made in God's likeness. Out of the same mouth come praise and cursing. My brothers and sisters, this should not be. Can both fresh water and salt water flow from the same spring? My brothers and sisters, can a fig tree bear olives, or a grapevine bear figs? Neither can a salt spring produce fresh water." James intensely illustrates the immense influence of our words. He uses the metaphor of a tiny flame capable of igniting a vast forest fire to emphasize the devastating consequences of unrestrained speech. This is a powerful reminder to always be quick to listen and slow to speak in conversations. We are given the power to change a heart, not break it. We are all guilty of this. We are flawed humans, but if we stop and ask the Holy Spirit to help us with our conversations, we will speak life over death.

Finally, let's look at a beautiful Scripture that we all can meditate on to help our spirits align with His. Colossians 4:6 says, "Let your conversation be always full of grace, seasoned with salt, so that you may know how to answer everyone." This verse is about communicating with both gentleness and insight, ensuring your words are beneficial and engaging, not dull or lifeless. Like salt, a believer's speech should be a valuable seasoning, both conserving and elevating the message of Christ. We must as believers continue to be gracious and allow the Holy Spirit to empower our conversations so we can speak life into others.

I remember when I was in a season of arrogance and self-promotion. This season was before I followed Jesus. I thought of myself as a Christian, but my actions and words were far from being those of an ambassador of Christ.

I would say things out of anger, malice, and selfish gain. I allowed pride to take center stage in my life. I easily let friends, coworkers, and family down by my better-than-you attitude and behavior. I was self-righteous and eager to let my voice be heard and my desires be met, no matter who it hurt. I have caused hearts to be broken and wounded. I lost many friends along the way. I am not proud of myself, and I only share to be raw and vulnerable with you. We are all sinners in need of a Savior. We lack the ability to do this life on our own. At some point, you will come to a place of absolute surrender and start living like you believe what you believe. Your life will begin to bear fruit, and you will be a voice of truth to those around you. I am a different person today than I once was. I am a living testimony of how divine intervention can bring lasting change and soften a hardened heart.

MAKING IT ABOUT ME

Message: *Season every conversation with grace.* Read the following Scriptures and meditate on these truths for a while. Let them simmer in your spirit before moving on.

Ephesians 4:29: "Do not let any unwholesome talk come out of your mouths, but only what is helpful for building others up according to their needs, that it may benefit those who listen."

James 3:9–12: "With the tongue we praise our Lord and Father, and with it we curse human beings, who have been made in God's likeness. Out of the same mouth come praise and cursing. My brothers and sisters, this should not be. Can both fresh water and salt water flow from the same spring? My brothers and sisters, can a fig tree bear olives, or a grapevine bear figs? Neither can a salt spring produce fresh water."

Colossians 4:6: "Let your conversation be always full of grace, seasoned with salt, so that you may know how to answer everyone."

Missional: Take a few moments and reflect on your living hope—Jesus. How has God been revealing Himself to you in your life?

Meditate: I pray you allow the Holy Spirit to work in and through you, bringing redemption and beauty into broken and dry places in your heart. May the Lord continue to speak truth into you so you will know how to live and speak life into the world around you, extinguishing flaming tongues and allowing the water of grace to penetrate thirsty and dying souls. Be salt and light to the world.

Heavenly Father,

Thank You for teaching me how to live and speak to those around me with grace and kindness. Forgive me when I lack and speak unwholesomely. Teach me to abide and bring glory and honor to You in all I say and do. You are the well and spring of life that flows in and through me.

In Jesus's name, Amen

HEARING HIS VOICE: THE HOLY SPIRIT AND YOUR JOURNEY OF FAITH

I encourage you to stop and slow down. Be still and listen to that still, small voice today—the voice of obedience, goodness, and wisdom. Be captivated by the Holy Spirit; He is the voice of truth.

Have you ever had a moment that just felt like all the stars aligned and you were in the right place at the right time? You know that feeling you get, and you say to yourself, *This can't be a coincidence,* and you wonder how this happened so perfectly and just at the right time. Those times when your prayers were answered or you had clarity through something someone said, and it was like they knew your thoughts or circumstances. Are you someone who believes in coincidences or divine intervention? Do you walk by faith or by sight? How do we live an abundant life in Christ with purpose and zeal for the kingdom of God? I believe the answer rests in your understanding of the third person of the Trinity—the Holy Spirit.

I had a very tangible encounter with the Holy Spirit, which set me on a journey to understand His character more fully. The Lord revealed so much to me through many teachings from various pastors, Bible scholars, and theologians. I have read and prayed through the Scriptures and enjoyed studying the character and depth of the Holy Spirit. The more time you spend in the Word, turning from sin, walking in obedience, and praying, the deeper your relationship with the Holy Spirit will become. He is your counselor and comforter in all things. The Holy Spirit guides you into all truth. Do you know that the Holy Spirit is the third person of the Trinity? He is not a force of nature. He can manifest Himself as fire, wind, and even a dove, but He is much more than that. The New Testament describes the Holy Spirit as having a mind (1 Cor. 2:10–11), a will (1 Cor. 12:11), and emotions (Eph. 4:30). These characteristics are typical of a person, not a neutral force.

First, let's look at the first time we receive the Holy Spirit. This happens when we are saved; the Holy Spirit dwells and resides in us. Ephesians 1:13–14 says, "And you also were included in Christ when you heard the message of truth, the gospel of your salvation. When you believed, you were marked in him with a seal, the promised Holy Spirit, who is a deposit guaranteeing our inheritance until the redemption of those who are God's possession—to the praise of his glory." Believing in Christ after hearing the gospel results in being marked by the Holy Spirit. This "seal" acts as God's guarantee of our promised inheritance in Christ, a spiritual sign of His ownership and security. Furthermore, the Bible tells us that the Holy Spirit is a distinct person within the Trinity, coequal with God the Father and God the Son. This divine presence actively operates in the world, specifically guiding, convicting, and empowering those who have faith. The Holy Spirit works through us, bestowing spiritual gifts and reshaping our character to reflect the fruit of the Spirit: love, joy, peace, patience, kindness, goodness, faithfulness, gentleness, and self-control. Once saved, you have the Holy Spirit. You may wonder how you can be empowered by the Holy Spirit and access your spiritual gifts.

One characteristic of the Holy Spirit is omnipresence. The omnipresence of God means He is everywhere at the same time. God is with every believer at once; He dwells within us. But the intimate workings of God in our lives are the manifest presence of God—the Holy Spirit upon us or filling us. When we are filled with the Holy Spirit, His influence in our lives grows, and we operate under the gifting of the Holy Spirit. Our minds are renewed daily and become more filled with the fruit of the Spirit. There is a difference between being sealed by the Holy Spirit and having Him rest upon you.

How do we allow the Holy Spirit to dwell on us and fill us daily? In Luke 3:16 (ESV), John the Baptist states, "I baptize you with water, but he who is mightier than I is coming, the strap of whose sandals I am not worthy to untie. He will baptize you with the Holy Spirit and fire." This passage tells us that the Messiah's baptism with the Holy Spirit and fire will be a more profound spiritual transformation than John's water baptism. This describes the divine empowerment where God's Spirit fills believers, enabling them to live a life of spiritual power and become effective witnesses and disciples. I can attest to this. I was baptized by water in my thirties. I started my journey of faith and began seeking the goodness of God. I was obedient and continued drawing near to God daily, building my relationship with Him through prayer and the disciplines of the faith. I began to change from the inside out. But it was not until I had a tangible experience of the presence of the Holy Spirit that I began to live my life on mission for the kingdom of God in all that I did. It was a holy fire baptism that transformed me and led me to repentance of all my past and present sins. It was the beginning of a life lived abundantly in Christ.

John 14:15–20 tells us:

> If you love me, keep my commands. And I will ask the Father, and he will give you another advocate to help you and be with you forever—the Spirit of truth. The world cannot accept him, because it neither sees him nor knows him. But you know him, for he lives with you and will be in you. I will not leave you as orphans; I will come to you. Before long, the world will not see me anymore, but you will see me. Because I live, you also will live. On that day you will realize that I am in my Father, and you are in me, and I am in you.

According to Jesus, love and obedience are essential; the Holy Spirit will come as promised, and God's presence remains with us. The Holy Spirit brings power and fire that enables and equips the believer to do the will of God. Acts 1:8 (ESV) says: "But you will receive power when the Holy Spirit has come upon you, and you will be my witnesses in Jerusalem and in all Judea and Samaria, and to the end of the earth." According to this verse, the power to witness is a gift of the Holy Spirit, not a product of human effort. This divine enablement equips believers to face challenges and effectively proclaim the gospel. To be "filled with the Holy Spirit" means you, the believer, must be fully surrendered to the Spirit's control and influence, allowing the Holy Spirit to direct and empower every part of your life. It's about more than just the Spirit's presence; it's actively yielding to His guidance and manifesting the fruit of the Spirit. The filling of the Spirit is an ongoing process of surrendering to the Holy Spirit's influence. The filling of the Spirit empowers believers to live lives that are pleasing to God, overcome temptation, and be filled with joy and peace. A Spirit-filled life is a life that is continuously dependent on and empowered by the Holy Spirit.

I can tell you many stories about divine interventions by the Holy Spirit. I can be sitting in church, and the pastor may speak about something I am going through, and the Scripture may align with the exact Scripture I read and meditated on that week. When I am reading a verse or a passage in the Bible, the Holy Spirit illuminates the Word, and it seems to just resonate and speak into my circumstance. God is alive and always speaks to us, mostly through His Word. I need to slow down, rest, and stop the busyness that surrounds me to hear His voice. It requires me to be still and spend time in prayer, reading His Word, and listening more than talking to the Lord. Set aside time to have intimacy and devotion to the Lord. He is always with us and is pursuing us. He is worthy of our time and attention.

If you become too busy, you will easily be prone to wander and ignore His still, small voice, and it will not come. The Holy Spirit is still there, but you can't hear Him because of your disobedience. It is a continuous walk and journey of faith. One thing I have learned on my journey is to be in biblical community with other believers. You need a spiritual "parent" to teach you and give you the wisdom of walking with Jesus. I have had the privilege to walk alongside some wise elders in my life. They have given me encouragement and wisdom that has deepened my faith. It is important to be in a solid, biblical, gospel-centered church to grow and learn how to be a disciple of Jesus. You need to pray and read your Bible daily and stop sipping the spiritual milk that others feed you. You need to start learning on your own with the Lord. The Holy Spirit will guide you. Start serving the world around you and using your time, treasures, and talents for the kingdom of God.

MAKING IT ABOUT ME

Message: *Listen to the voice of truth.* Read the following Scriptures and meditate on these truths for a while. Let them simmer in your spirit before moving on.

Ephesians 1:13–14: "And you also were included in Christ when you heard the message of truth, the gospel of your salvation. When you believed, you were marked in him with a seal, the promised Holy Spirit, who is a deposit guaranteeing our inheritance until the redemption of those who are God's possession—to the praise of his glory."

Luke 3:16 (ESV): "I baptize you with water, but he who is mightier than I is coming, the strap of whose sandals I am not worthy to untie. He will baptize you with the Holy Spirit and fire."

John 14:15–20: "If you love me, keep my commands. And I will ask the Father, and he will give you another advocate to help you and be with you forever—the Spirit of truth. The world cannot accept him, because it neither sees him nor knows him. But you know him, for he lives with you and will be in you. I will not leave you as orphans; I will come to you. Before long, the world will not see me anymore, but you will see me. Because I live, you also will live. On that day you will realize that I am in my Father, and you are in me, and I am in you."

Acts 1:8 (ESV): "But you will receive power when the Holy Spirit has come upon you, and you will be my witnesses in Jerusalem and in all Judea and Samaria, and to the end of the earth."

Missional: Take a few moments and abide and let the Holy Spirit guide you into His truth. Are you plugged into a local church and biblical community to help you grow spiritually? Do you spend time with the Spirit of God listening and asking for guidance and direction in your life? Where have you seen the Holy Spirit work in your life?

Meditate: I pray you reflect on your journey of faith today. Be still with the Holy Spirit and let Him guide you into all truth.

Heavenly Father,

Thank You for the gift of the Holy Spirit and His power working in and through me to bring You glory. Help me to abide in You. You are my salvation.

In Jesus's name, Amen

DAY 4

PRAISE THROUGH THE
PAIN: FINDING PURPOSE
IN SUFFERING

I want to encourage you today to keep going, no matter how hard things seem or how difficult your circumstances feel. Trust the process, relinquish your control, and let the Lord fight your battles. Be still in the waiting.

Do you try to control each step of your life? Are you allowing others to dictate your outcomes? Do you fight your battles in your own strength and will, creating the drama around you by going to others for advice rather than to God? Are you weary from your continued striving for everything to be perfect, or setting high expectations on others, or the end results of your circumstances? Do you allow the Holy Spirit to work in and through you during the process, not letting those around you that are causing stress or discouragement lead you to grumble or worse, create more havoc and destruction? I know I struggle with this, and I have found that if I let go and trust the Lord with the outcome, it is always better than if I rush and attempt to create my desired outcome. We face trials and tribulations every day. It is how we handle the process that determines our reaction and response through the trial.

Let's look at the book of Job. Job was a righteous and faithful man of God. "This man was blameless and upright; he feared God and shunned evil" (Job 1:1). He was a wealthy, honorable, and devout man. He suffered and endured immense loss of possessions, family, and health, all planned by Satan, who claimed Job's devotion to the Lord was motivated by His blessings rather

235

than genuine faith. In spite of these trials, Job refuses to curse God, though he questions his suffering. I know we have all been guilty of questioning why we must suffer, especially when we are amid the pain. It sometimes feels like God is silent or absent during the struggle. We can oftentimes feel that we are being punished for something when the trial is beyond our human understanding. We want relief and an end to the suffering. We may question why a good God would allow trials and tribulations to occur.

God allowed Satan to test Job's faith. Job refused to curse God through every immense trial. He remained faithful to God. Job's friends tried comforting him, but their arguments accused Job of having hidden sins that must be the cause of his suffering. Job's suffering leads him to question God's justice, but God's intercession reveals that human understanding is limited and God's ways are not always clear to us. God's ways are higher than ours, and He works everything out for our good. Job is eventually humbled and realizes the power and wisdom of God. The Lord restores Job's life and blesses him. The book of Job delves into the complex nature of suffering, the need for trusting divine wisdom, and the importance of unwavering faith amid hardship. It stands as an example of human strength and belief when confronted with the unfathomable.

I have faced trials of many kinds in my life. I can remember oftentimes feeling just like Job, thinking to myself, *How can this be happening to me? I am a faithful woman of God. This surely must be a punishment.* I would question whether God was listening to my pleas. Each trial I faced allowed me to see God's handiwork once the trial had passed. Often, we realize how God was working it out once we stop and reflect. There is always a blessing, a restoration, or a refining moment. The Lord is always with us and is working it out for our good and His glory. He is faithful. I know that for me, I no longer question the reason why I am facing a trial, no matter how intense the struggle or how long I must endure it. I know there is purpose and power in the pain. I am learning to praise through the waiting, allowing the Lord to fight my battles while I remain still in Him. I have faith that the Lord is teaching and refining me to be more like Him. I pray you keep the faith amid pain and suffering, and you continue to do good and persevere. Galatians 6:9 tells us, "Let us not become weary in doing good, for at the proper time we will reap a harvest if we do not give up."

The Lord is good, and we must continue to walk in faith, living out God's promises. Keep shining and doing good to those around you. He sees, He is good, and He will make all things new in His glorious timing.

MAKING IT ABOUT ME

Message: *There is purpose in your suffering.* Read the following Scriptures and meditate on these truths for a while. Let them simmer in your spirit before moving on.

> Job 1:1: "This man was blameless and upright; he feared God and shunned evil."

> Galatians 6:9: "Let us not become weary in doing good, for at the proper time we will reap a harvest if we do not give up."

Missional: Take a few minutes and reflect on the goodness in your life. What are you struggling with today? How do you see God working in your life to bring you to a refining moment or season? Write down how God has been faithful to His promises in your life.

Meditate: I pray you continue to draw near to the Lord in your trials and sufferings. He is faithful and will work everything out for your good and His glory.

Heavenly Father,

Thank You for being so faithful to me in the midst of my pain.
I long for Your presence and comfort as I walk through the valley
of the shadow of death. Lead me to Your still waters where
I am safe. Help me to abide and be still in Your presence.

In Jesus's name, Amen

UNSHAKABLE JOY: FINDING YOUR STRENGTH IN GOD'S PURPOSE

I want to encourage you today to focus on the joy set before you in Jesus. There is a purpose and a plan that is destined and waiting for you. Walk in the promises of God and let nothing steal your joy. You are the light to the world around you, and the darkness can't hold you back. Are you living for the people around you rather than for what God has destined and planned for you? Are you worried about pleasing others more than God? Are your priorities fleeting and your mind fixated on the goal of your daily happiness, or are you living missionally and serving the world around you with peace and contentment in every circumstance? Do you wake up ready to bless others in your day, whether the circumstances align with your happiness or not? Does it feel like every effort you make to stay positive has a counterproductive enemy ready to attack and thwart your plans, ultimately stealing your joy? Do you let others control your peace? Does your joy and strength come from the Lord?

"The joy of the Lord is your strength" comes from Nehemiah 8:10. It indicates that true strength and resilience are derived from the joy found in a relationship with God, not from circumstantial happiness. When we focus our minds on joy, we gain supernatural strength only found in our walk with Jesus. You may be wondering how we can sustain our joy when the surrounding circumstances seem to steal our peace and leave us feeling overwhelmed and discouraged. Psalm 16:11 says, "You make known to me the path of life; you will fill me with joy in your presence, with eternal pleasures at your right hand." This verse emphasizes the importance of being near to the Lord. His presence brings abundant joy and internal peace that will lead us to walk in our kingdom purpose and destiny. Walking in agreement with God's will ultimately leads us to a life filled with joy and contentment in every circumstance. Life has many moments of happiness that are pleasing and satisfying to our flesh, but these can be fleeting. The euphoria of happiness does not last forever and often changes with our circumstances. Life has a way of derailing us and leaving us feeling empty when things don't go the way we have planned. We can easily allow the pain and defeat to lead us to wander down the path of regret, sorrow, and disappointment. The course of our day can leave us shattered and empty if we let it.

I am currently in a situation that has me trusting the Lord as I walk in faith, not knowing the outcome. I am letting God lead my steps toward His purposes for me. It requires me to draw near to the Lord with every step, knowing He is my strength. This is not an easy process. My flesh wants to give up and go back to what is familiar and comfortable. Stepping out of my comfort zone and self-will can be hard, but when we move with God's will and purposes for us, they will not fail, and we will have lasting peace. I walk in obedience toward the unknown, but I walk with the Lord, and I know His plans are higher and are predestined for me to bring Him glory.

Finally, 1 Thessalonians 5:16–18 says, "Rejoice always, pray continually, give thanks in all circumstances; for this is God's will for you in Christ Jesus." This passage clearly tells us we should pray unceasingly, be thankful in all things, and have a foundation in joy rooted in faith. We must draw near to God and trust that His plans are bigger and better than we could have ever asked or imagined for ourselves. The Lord will lead us to a life filled with peace and thankfulness that draws from the strength only found in the joy of the Lord.

MAKING IT ABOUT ME

Message: *We can have unshakable joy in the Lord.* Read the following Scriptures and meditate on these truths for a while. Let them simmer in your spirit before moving on.

Nehemiah 8:10: "The joy of the LORD is your strength."

1 Thessalonians 5:16–18: "Rejoice always, pray continually, give thanks in all circumstances; for this is God's will for you in Christ Jesus."

Missional: Take a few moments and reflect on all the gifts in your life. Let the joy of the Lord wash over you and write all the things you are thankful for today.

Meditate: I pray you find peace knowing your joy comes from the Lord. He is your strength, and He has a plan and a destiny that only you can fulfill. Draw near to the Lord today.

Heavenly Father,

Thank You for being my strength in every season of my life. I draw from Your pillar of strength and find contentment knowing You are sovereign over me. You are my strong tower and my peace.

In Jesus's name, Amen

YOUR UNFOLDING STORY: A LIFE LIVED FOR HIS KINGDOM

I want to encourage you today to cling to the Lord in all that you do. Be thankful and worship the Lord with reverence and awe. He sees you, and He loves you. Jesus is with you every step of your journey. His love endures forever.

Do you ever feel like you are not worthy of God's love? Have you ever had thoughts of doubt or shame come upon you because you feel like you are not living up to a righteous standard or religious belief? Do you tell yourself you are not good enough to be loved or forgiven? Do you put up walls around your emotions and lash out when those walls begin to crack and are shaken? Do you have thoughts of doubt or defeat? Are you struggling to understand how to navigate a world that seems doomed for destruction with no hope in sight? Is your kingdom shaking?

These are questions we all grapple with as we journey through life. We face many hardships and pitfalls along the way. This can leave us feeling alone and defeated, wondering why this is happening, or worse, *Why is a good person like me going through this when I have faith and believe in a good God?*

Romans 8:1 tells us, "Therefore, there is now no condemnation for those who are in Christ Jesus." If you put your trust in Jesus, there is freedom from the consequences of sin. This does not mean that even though our debt is paid, we should continue living recklessly. We should be more apt to live life abundantly in Christ because of what He has done for us. The love of Jesus is a love that is unconditional and worthy of all our praise. This love is not a fleshly love but a deep, holy kind of love not defined by worldly standards. If you love Jesus, you cannot love the things of this world.

First John 2:15–17 tells us: "Do not love the world or anything in the world. If anyone loves the world, love for the Father is not in them. For everything in the world—the lust of the flesh, the lust of the eyes, and the pride of life—comes not from the Father but from the world. The world and its desires pass away, but whoever does the will of God lives forever." We are called to do the will of the Father and to live for His kingdom purposes. We cannot be double-minded people living for the world and for the kingdom of God. Pursuing what brings goodness and mercy to others and living out God's promises will lead you to a life lived in abundance in Christ.

I recently was listening to a sermon, and the pastor talked about how we know we love God. We have a passion to pursue His glory. We are not loving through an emotion but through action, pursuing things that will bring God glory. This love is sacrificial and pursues kingdom purposes.

We each have a story that God is unfolding in our lives. We are on a journey of faith, and we get to play a part in other God stories, which is a privilege and a blessing. We are meant to journey together, sharing our experiences and giving the hope that we received through our own trials and tribulations. Our pain is someone else's medicine, bringing strength and a deeper faith as we navigate this life together.

I went to a conference many years ago, and in my chair, tucked in the program pamphlet, was a Scripture. This Scripture was prayed over my life by someone I have never met. I have kept that Scripture in my Bible ever since. On occasion, the Lord uses it to strengthen me on my walk with Him. It is Hebrews 12:28–29: "Therefore, since we are receiving a kingdom that cannot be shaken, let us be thankful, and so worship God acceptably with reverence and awe, for our 'God is a consuming fire.'" We are called to be thankful with reverence and awe, giving the Lord our acceptable worship.

With the uncertainty of this world, believers are encouraged to find strength and stability in a kingdom that cannot be shaken. Our response is to worship. Worship in the pain. Worship in the victory. Worship in the waiting. The Lord has a purpose and a plan for our lives that He is orchestrating to bring us to our kingdom destiny.

MAKING IT ABOUT ME

Message: *We are receiving an unshakable kingdom.* Read the following Scriptures and meditate on these truths for a while. Let them simmer in your spirit before moving on.

Romans 8:1: "Therefore, there is now no condemnation for those who are in Christ Jesus."

1 John 2:15–17: "Do not love the world or anything in the world. If anyone loves the world, love for the Father is not in them. For everything in the world—the lust of the flesh, the lust of the eyes, and the pride of life—comes not from the Father but from the world. The world and its desires pass away, but whoever does the will of God lives forever."

Hebrews 12:28–29: "Therefore, since we are receiving a kingdom that cannot be shaken, let us be thankful, and so worship God acceptably with reverence and awe, for our 'God is a consuming fire.'"

Missional: Take a few moments and relish the awe and goodness of God. He is an unstoppable force in your life. He is pursuing you and is a consuming fire. How has your faith been refined? What are some areas that need reshaping to be more kingdom focused and driven?

_____

_____

_____

Meditate: I pray you find strength in the waiting. Your story is being written. If you are still breathing, God is not done with you yet. You have a purpose that only you can fulfill. The Lord loves you and wants you to pursue His kingdom and His will for your life. Trust the process.

Heavenly Father,

Thank You for pursuing me and transforming me to be more like You. I trust You in the waiting because I know You are working everything out for my good. You are my strength, and You are worthy of all honor, glory, and praise.

In Jesus's name, Amen

ROAD TO PURPOSE: YOUR KINGDOM DESTINY AWAITS

I want to encourage you to continue on the path that is set before you. Let Jesus take your wheel. Sit back and trust in His steady hand as He guides you down every gravel turn and every shift-in-the-dirt detour to the providential road to purpose, leading straight to your kingdom destiny.

Are you a backseat driver in your life? Are you taking control of the GPS and map, telling God how and where to drive you? It is time to let God steer the wheel and trust Him to bring you to the narrow road less traveled. Did you know you were created with a God-given purpose and destiny, predestined to be revealed by God? Psalm 139:16 says, "Your eyes saw my unformed body; all the days ordained for me were written in your book before one of them came to be." This verse conveys that God has a plan and orchestrates your life at conception, that your life is predestined. Your life's path has been planned with a purpose. You are not traveling through life without a destination.

Ephesians 1:11 (ESV) says, "In him we have obtained an inheritance, having been predestined according to the purpose of him who works all things according to the counsel of his will." This verse calls attention to God having a specific purpose for each person that He is working to bring to fruition. You can rest, knowing that Jesus is working everything out and is leading you to your kingdom destiny.

We are on a journey of faith, and each season of life has a purpose, leading us to live lives that are holy and pleasing to God, ultimately leading us to our kingdom destiny. Ecclesiastes 3:1 says: "There is a time for everything, and a season for every activity under the heavens." This verse reminds us that just as there are seasons, life has different stages, and God has a reason for every period we experience. He drives us to our purpose.

I have been through many difficult seasons in my life that have shaped the woman I am today. I have traveled down roads that led me to dead ends or places off the beaten path. I have spun my "vehicle" out of control, trying to grip the steering wheel of life so tightly I lost control and ended up in dark ditches that left me in critical situations. But once I surrendered my control and let Jesus be the driver of my life and take the wheel, He led me back on the road to recovery, redemption, and grace. He steered me to the straight and narrow path, the providential road to my purpose, leading me to my kingdom destiny.

MAKING IT ABOUT ME

Message: *You have a providential road to purpose.* Read the following Scriptures and meditate on these truths for a while. Let them simmer in your spirit before moving on.

> Psalm 139:16: "Your eyes saw my unformed body; all the days ordained for me were written in your book before one of them came to be."

> Ephesians 1:11 (ESV): "In him we have obtained an inheritance, having been predestined according to the purpose of him who works all things according to the counsel of his will."

> Ecclesiastes 3:1: "There is a time for everything, and a season for every activity under the heavens."

Missional: Take a few moments and reflect on your journey of faith. Are you living with a kingdom mindset and living out your God-given kingdom purpose? Write down your vision and the road you see yourself on as Jesus takes the wheel.

Meditate: I pray you let Jesus take the wheel on your journey of faith down the unwinding road to your kingdom destiny.

Heavenly Father,

Thank You for being the driver of my life. Jesus, take the wheel and lead me to the providential road to Your kingdom purpose and destiny for my life. You are the author and finisher of my faith.

In Jesus's name, Amen

CONCLUSION

Do you ever wonder why the valleys of life can seem so lonely and feel like they're never going to end? Do your cries for help from the Lord ever feel like they're not being answered or even heard? Do you only call upon the Lord in the seasons of despair? Are you praising the Lord only in the high times of life? Those times when your cup runs over? Are you someone that tends to only seek God for self-gratification, ultimately looking for your will, not His? These are tough questions all of us probably have wrestled with at different seasons of life. You are human, and it is normal to feel this way at times on your journey of faith, but the key is not to stay in those spaces too long and to always give thanks in every circumstance.

Have you called upon the Lord lately just to thank Him and say you love Him? Just to be in His presence with no agenda? I encourage you to do that today and more often. Rest in His presence. I have been spending more time lately reflecting on my own walk and seeking God's will and considering how I can be a catalyst for change in not only my inner circle but those circles beyond my reach. I have a stirring in my heart to encourage and share the Lord's goodness with those around me every day. I find myself asking and seeking the Lord's will daily, trusting in His promises for me even when the circumstances seem challenging or difficult. I am praising anyway. I am currently studying the book of Isaiah. This Scripture was one I came across in my studies last week, and it resonated with me again. Isaiah 6:8–10 tells us:

> Then I heard the voice of the Lord saying, "Whom shall I send? And who will go for us?"

And I said, "Here am I. Send me!"

He said, "Go and tell this people:

'Be ever hearing, but never understanding;

be ever seeing, but never perceiving.'

Make the heart of this people calloused;

make their ears dull

and close their eyes.

Otherwise they might see with their eyes,

hear with their ears,

understand with their hearts,

and turn and be healed."

The Bible Project explains that God tells Isaiah to deliver a message of judgment to the people of Judah, but this message will not be received as a call to repentance. Instead, the people will reject the message, harden their hearts, become spiritually deaf and blind, and consequently experience judgment through exile. However, this act of judgment will also preserve a "holy seed" (a remnant) through which God's plan for redemption will eventually be fulfilled. That "holy seed" will come and bring life, light, and freedom to the world for those that repent and turn from their wicked ways, ask for forgiveness of their sins, and accept the Son of Man, Jesus, as Lord and Savior of their life. As believers, we have a call to be sent. To be the light in the darkness. We all have a story or testimony that would benefit another person who may be struggling with the same thing. We all have a kingdom purpose and destiny that will glorify God. Our goal in life should be to make heaven crowded. Where is God calling you today? It could be to a neighbor, a friend, a coworker, a family member, a stranger, or even an enemy. God could be calling you to a mission field far from home, or your mission field may be in your own home or community.

I am reminded of Philippians 2:13: "For it is God who works in you to will and to act in order to fulfill his good purpose."

It takes God's power and strength working in and through us to fulfill His plans for our lives. May we continue fighting the good fight and seeking the Lord in all that we do and sharing with those in our inner circle the goodness of God.

I pray that you cling to your faith and thank the Lord for each moment and breath, praising and thanking Him for all the good things in your life. May you hear the call of the Lord and say yes to where the Lord sends you.

I wrote "The Power of Your Pain" (Week 6, Day 1) three weeks after assassination of Charlie Kirk. My heart was heavy over this brave young man that died too soon. Charlie Kirk had a kingdom mindset and a greater calling and purpose. He lived his life on mission for Jesus. He was wise beyond his years and had an unextinguishable Holy Spirit–filled kind of fire. He spoke truth with love and grace. His words had deep conviction, and he never sugarcoated sin to those that debated his beliefs. I loved watching his debates and speeches that kept the hard conversations going. I always walked away feeling inspired and educated. It provoked my spirit to keep teaching the gospel and continue encouraging my circles of influence. Charlie Kirk stated with much conviction, "Jesus defeated death so you could live." May you continue to live the life you were called to live.

Romans 8:28 tells us, "And we know that in all things God works for the good of those who love him, who have been called according to his purpose." My prayer is that Charlie Kirk's voice and mission continue through the body of Christ. We must rise up and be bold in our faith, even when the conversation is difficult, and love with grace and humility. My mission in life has not changed: I live for the kingdom of God, proclaiming truth with everyone I meet.

We have come to the end of our journey together. It is time to finish the last sip of your coffee or tea and get up and start your new beginning. My hope and prayer for you is that you spend time seeking and learning from the teachings of Jesus. Your life is not by chance. I believe you did not pick up this book by accident. I have prayed for you as we journeyed together through these pages. I am not a theologian, pastor, or scholar, but I am a woman who had an encounter with Jesus that changed everything. I have tasted and seen that the Lord is good, and I want to share the love of Jesus with everyone. I am a nobody, but with Jesus I am somebody through Him, telling everybody about what He has done for me. You may be on the road to salvation, the road to recovery and redemption, or the long road to obedience. Each of these roads leads you to the road to providential purpose leading you to your kingdom destiny.

ABOUT THE AUTHOR

A heart for the classroom, a soul for the Word. Welcome to a community Rooted in Christ's Love. Monika Harrison believes that every season of life is a classroom. After a successful first act in the business world, she followed a calling into education, discovering a passion for making complex truths simple and applicable. "I believe the Lord's Providence led me out of corporate world and into the classroom, where my real ministry as a teacher began." This unique blend of professional leadership and an educative heart define her writing, offering readers a roadmap that is both practical and spiritually grounded.

Monika is a dedicated educator and Biblical life coach committed to strengthening the Body of Christ through impactful ministry and scriptural-based teaching. Today, she serves as a first-grade teacher, holding a degree in Early Childhood Education. Beyond the classroom, Monika has spent over 10 years in counseling and recovery ministry. Her commitment to seeing lives transformed is backed by Biblical Life Coaching certificates from Light University. This unique blend of educational expertise and soulful guidance allows her to see the "whole person"— whether she is helping a six-year-old learn to read or walking alongside a woman on her spiritual journey. Through her work and her message,

The Providential Road to Purpose, she is honored to walk alongside others to help them grow deeper in their relationship with Jesus.

A faithful servant at her local church, she is deeply involved in the community. She finds great joy in:

- **Leading Women's Bible Studies**: Creating safe spaces for women to dive deep into Scripture and find healing.

- **Recovery Advocacy**: Using her decade of experience to support those navigating life's hardest seasons.

- **Mentorship**: Bridging the gap between biblical principles and everyday life.

Whether she is teaching phonics or facilitating a small group, Monika's mission remains the same: to reflect the light of Christ and empower others to live out their God-given purpose.

Monika Harrison is the author of *Providential Road to Purpose* and the visionary behind Women Rooted in Love. With a heart for helping women navigate the complexities of faith and calling, she writes to illuminate the divine fingerprints on every life story. Through her work, she seeks to bridge the gap between feeling lost and finding one's place in God's plan. When she isn't writing or ministering to her community, Monika can be found running to her favorite worship music, reading her Bible while enjoying her favorite cup of coffee, and spending time with her husband, Steve, and two children, Joshua and Jasmine.

· · ·

Monika invites you to discover your *Providential Road to Purpose* and join a community of **Women Rooted in Christ's Love** at

WWW.WOMENROOTEDINLOVE.COM